D1288097

The Big Book of Balloons

The Big Book of Balloons

CREATE ALMOST ANYTHING
FOR EVERY PARTY AND HOLIDAY

**Text and Illustrations
by Captain Visual**

A Citadel Press Book
Published by Carol Publishing Group

A Citadel Press Book
Published by Carol Publishing Group
Citadel Press is a registered trademark of Carol Communications, Inc.
Editorial, sales and distribution, and rights and permissions inquiries should be addressed to Carol Publishing Group, 120 Enterprise Avenue, Secaucus, N.J. 07094.

In Canada: Canadian Manda Group, One Atlantic Avenue, Suite 105, Toronto, Ontario M6K 3E7

Carol Publishing Group books may be purchased in bulk at special discounts for sales promotion, fund-raising, or educational purposes. Special editions can be created to specifications. For details, contact: Special Sales Department, Carol Publishing Group, 120 Enterprise Avenue, Secaucus, N.J. 07094.

Designed by Andrew B. Gardner

Manufactured in the United States of America

10   9   8   7   6   5   4   3   2   1

Library of Congress Cataloging-in-Publication Data

Captain Visual.
[Big book of balloons]
    The big book of balloons : create almost anything for every party and holiday / Captain Visual.
        p. cm.
    "A Citadel Press book."
    ISBN 0-8065-1920-7 (pbk.)
    1. Balloons sculpture. 2. Balloon decorations. 3. Holiday decorations. I. Title.
TT926.C373 1997
745.594—dc21
                                                            97-20751
                                                            CIP

Dedication

To my beautiful wife Shari and our wonderful children Jenna and Michael, who are always in my heart. Through you I find inspiration, encouragement, and laughter. I love you all.

CONTENTS

ACKNOWLEDGMENTS

The art of balloon sculpting has existed for decades. It is, I believe, actually a told art because it has a long tradition of being taught more by word of mouth than by the written word. No matter how good any book or instruction sheet may be, nothing can replace actually seeing a balloon twisted and sculpted into a figure or design. Being able to hold the end result and examine its construction is irreplaceable for a student of the art.

Balloon art has literally been handed down from generous teachers to astute students who, in turn, continue to pass along their new ideas. Because of this rich sharing of techniques and ideas, balloon art has flourished from the simple balloon dog to the pinacles of the imagination.

My thanks go out to anyone who has passed along their kind assistance and inspiration because they have created the huge pool of possibility that I refer to constantly for concepts and inspiration.

Many designs have become classics that any student should know. These designs will appear in these pages at times, although their originators are unknown to me, to those pioneers I extend a special thanks for the clarity of vision that helped establish the foundations of this craft.

Let me also thank those that continue to create and share, for you are the key to the future of balloon art.

Finally, let me thank my wife Shari, whose support, encouragement, and diligence—both as my spouse and partner in clowning, as Hoopla the clown—enables me to share my ideas through this book and our work as entertainers.

INTRODUCTION

Holidays are for celebrating, and, as far as I'm concerned, no celebration is complete without balloons. It seems that from the time we are born, we are first introduced to balloons by the pink and blue balloons that greet us at the hospital and at our homecoming. Sure enough, balloons will be an integral part of nearly every birthday celebration to follow.

Balloons come out in all shapes and sizes for christenings, bar and bas mitzvahs, graduations, showers, weddings, retirements, holidays, and any other celebration that arises. Their brilliant colors, voluptuous shapes, and buoyant characteristics add a unique dimension to any event.

A balloon is a novelty, in and of itself. Merely a small rubber bag, inflated with air or helium, expanded to its limit without bursting, a balloon is an irresistible, yet fragile, toy. Simplicity is possibly its most endearing quality; a balloon bounces, bobs, and floats in the air. Tied to a string, it gains a petlike status, adored, treasured, and cared for by its master.

The short life of a balloon makes the moments spent with it that much more precious, especially for children who naturally grieve for balloons that escape to Balloon Heaven or meet an untimely demise after contact with an unforgiving sharp object.

Recently, new ways have been found to generate excitement with balloons. Balloons are now clustered to form bouquets, and are delivered just like flowers. They are used for decorations, assembled en masse to form large sculptures, structures, and signs. They are released to float or to drop, creating excitement at events.

Most notably, as you will see in this book, they are twisted, squeezed, locked, and sometimes, even popped (where appropriate, in some places), and combined to form delicate, colorful, sometimes intricate designs or sculptures that can be used decoratively or as toys. These activities are commonly referred to as Balloon Sculpting or

Balloon Art. Blessed with such versatility and vivacious qualities, it is no wonder that balloons are a must at *any* celebration.

Balloon Sculpting truly opens the doors to endless possibilities of creating with balloons. Throughout this book, various twisting, or sculpting, techniques will be described, each establishing itself as a type of building block that can be incorporated with other techniques to create beautiful holiday designs.

In the past Balloon Art was popularized by the sculpting of balloon animals, most notably dogs, rabbits, giraffes, bears, and swans. These and scores of other designs are thoroughly described in my first book, *Captain Visual's Big Book of Balloon Art,* a complete book of balloonology for beginners and advanced twisters that is currently available from Citadel Press.

Balloon animals, of course, only begin to skim the surface of what can be designed with balloons. Using holidays as a springboard, we are about to dive into a seemingly bottomless pool of exciting designs for which you will find practical use as the holidays of the calendar year unfold. From New Year's to Christmas, a parade of holidays and celebrations inspire colorful designs that will allow you to grow as a balloon artist, becoming aware of your own ideas and designs.

Beginners and experts will be able to find value in the following pages. Definitely, everyone will discover that when it comes to balloon art, every day can be a holiday! Keep Twistin'!

The Big Book of Balloons

Chapter One
Balloon Basics

Nearly everyone has seen and held a balloon, yet I am always amazed at how mystified people are when they see one twisted into a design, believing that it is some type of "special" balloon. Since balloons, with the exception of those constructed of Mylar, are all made of some type of latex rubber, they all share similar properties.

They are produced in a variety of shapes: some round, long, fat, skinny, wavy, big, and small. Some are preshaped as figures, like hearts, flowers, animal heads, ribbed worms, and clown bodies. Often balloons are produced with printing on them: of faces, bodies, patterns, and advertising.

Shape is the most important factor in deciding which balloon is right for the designs that you will be creating. Though it is possible to find creative uses for any shaped balloon, the most versatile shape has proven to be the long, skinny balloons known as animal, pencil, or twisty balloons. The most commonly used balloon of this type is technically known as the 260 (the number describes its shape when inflated, which is approximately two inches wide by sixty inches long).

"260"

Because balloon art has been increasing in popularity, it has become easier to find the 260's in stores. Party stores, magic shops, toy stores, and sometimes supermarkets are good places to look. Generally, 260's are sold by the gross (144 per bag). They are readily available from balloon suppliers through the mail. (A brief list of suppliers can be found at the back of this book.)

When you make your purchase, carefully read the warnings on the bag. Most manufacturers warn against inflating balloons by mouth and giving balloons to small children. If you buy balloons with no warning, please be smart and remember that all balloons and balloon fragments are extremely dangerous if swallowed or inhaled and can

choke anyone. Be sure to always keep your working area clear of any broken or discarded balloons.

As you begin to buy larger quantities of balloons, you may wish to store them in a cool, dark spot. The latex that composes balloons is biodegradable and will eventually break down, causing the balloon to become brittle and, more likely, to burst. Two elements that will accelerate the decomposition of your balloons are light and heat. Basements, closets, coolers, cardboard boxes, and refrigerators are all good places to store balloons.

Inflating your balloon is the most important part of shaping your balloon. Air that is forced by pressure into the balloon causes it to expand to the desired shape. Because it is not recommended to inflate balloons by mouth, finding a pump that you are comfortable with is important. This book comes with a small pump to get you started. Other pumps such as hand pumps, basketball pumps, and electric pumps are available in stores and through the list of suppliers at the back of this book. Experiment to find the pump that best suits your needs.

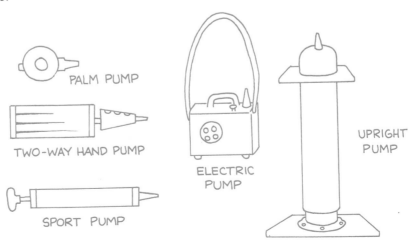

PALM PUMP

TWO-WAY HAND PUMP

SPORT PUMP

ELECTRIC PUMP

UPRIGHT PUMP

Long balloons expand from end to end, creating what is referred to as a tail when they are partially inflated. The inflated portion of the balloon is known as the body. The opening of the balloon is referred to as the mouth.

MOUTH   BODY   TAIL

The amount of air that you put into the balloon will determine how many bubbles you can twist into your balloon. You will find that with each twist, the tail of your balloon will become smaller as air is displaced into it. Eventually no tail will be present as you near the end of your design. Continued twisting once the tail is gone will result in a burst balloon. A good rule to follow is the more you intend to twist, the less air you should use to inflate the balloon.

Slide the mouth of the balloon over the nozzle of the pump. Continue holding the mouth to the nozzle so the pressure of the air does not blow the balloon off the pump. Fill the balloon with the desired amount of air, then remove the balloon from the pump while pinching the mouth closed with your fingers to prevent air from escaping.

After the balloon is inflated, you may wish to release a small amount of air. This action, known as "burping" the balloon, reduces the air pressure in the newly formed body of the balloon, relaxing it so that it is less likely to burst.

Now that the balloon is inflated, tying the knot at the mouth of the balloon will prevent the air from escaping. Pinch the neck of the balloon so the air cannot escape. With your other hand, stretch the mouth away from the body of the balloon, and create a loop around one or two of the fingers doing the pulling. Cross the stretched area over itself, and tuck the mouth of the balloon back through the opening in the loop. Pull gently on the mouth of the balloon, tightening the knot. Do not pull the knot too tight or you may damage the balloon.

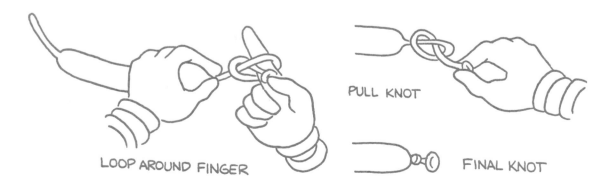

LOOP AROUND FINGER   PULL KNOT   FINAL KNOT

There is no wrong way to tie the knot. If you have a way that works better for you, use it!

Once you have inflated your balloon and tied a knot in it, play with it. Pinch it, squeeze it, bend it. Get comfortable with how the balloon feels and how far you can go with manipulating it. Learn not to be afraid of a balloon breaking. Know that it may indeed break, but that could be due to defects that the balloon may have developed from manufacturing or decomposition. It is a good idea to examine the bal-

TIRED BALLOON

loon for defects before inflating; this saves you time, frustration, and risk of injury.

You will notice that after you have worked with your balloon a while it will have lost some of its elasticity, and the body of the balloon will no longer have a tight feel to it. You have worn it out, like an old

TENSO THE CLOWN

pair of socks. Your balloon is "tired." A tired balloon is no good for twisting designs. It no longer has enough tension to hold bubbles, twists, and locks. It doesn't even *look* bright and cheery anymore.

Remember this as you practice. You may overwork a balloon trying to learn a new design, and it will no longer respond to your needs. Make note of your progress and start again with a new balloon.

By now you may have worn out a few balloons and are comfortable with their feel. More important, hopefully you have fewer fears of the balloon breaking. I believe that balloons can sense your tension when you are afraid, and they break under that pressure. So remember this rule: **RELAX.**

BUBBLES

A key part of balloon designing is the bubble. Every design consists of bubbles that are twisted into the balloon and arranged to form a figure. Bubbles can be made in an assortment of sizes, all determined by their length. Bubbles that are up to two inches in length tend to be round, while longer bubbles are more oval or tubelike.

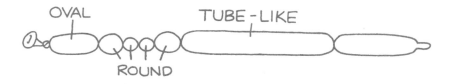

PINCH TWISTS

First, determine the size that you want your bubble to be. At the point where the bubble is to end, gently squeeze the balloon with your forefinger and thumb of one hand, and with your other hand twist the remaining portion of the balloon at least three times. The point where the twist is made is called a joint. Continue holding the new bubble and the rest of the balloon in place or your new bubble will untwist.

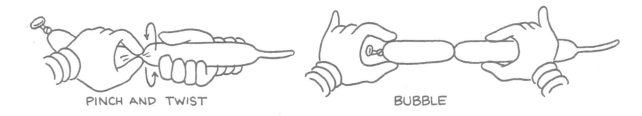

Continue holding the new bubble with your last two fingers and palm of your hand. With your free forefinger and thumb pinch your next bubble and twist again. As long as you continue holding the first bubble and the last bubble (which is usually the untwisted, remaining body of the balloon), you can make any number of bubbles, and they will not untwist, provided that you have twisted each bubble a sufficient number of times. A row of bubbles is called a chain.

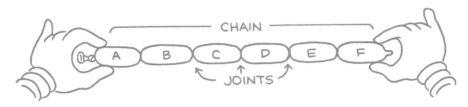

LOCK TWISTS

You do not want to walk around holding bubbles all day. The way to secure your new chain of bubbles is with a lock twist. To make a lock twist, align the joint of the first bubble with the joint of the last bubble and twist the two together. Remember to twist at least three times. The friction of the two bubbles against each other and the tension created by stretching the joints causes the bubbles to stay locked together.

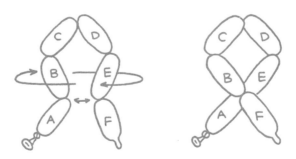

Here is a look at some regularly used chains after they have been lock twisted.

You can lock several balloons to each other by creating joints in each balloon and locking them together.

Another way of locking balloons together is to align the balloons at the point where they are to be joined, squeeze the balloons at this point, and then twist. This saves a step by not forming the joints initially.

You may also use this technique when working with one balloon as shown on page 8. This is often referred to as a fold twist.

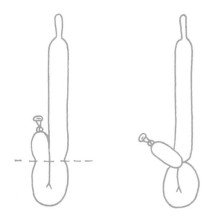

All balloon designs are the result of an assembly of twists and lock twists. Though there are many more techniques to be learned, these are the most fundamental. You are now prepared to begin sculpting.

Below are examples of lock twists used to lock one balloon together.

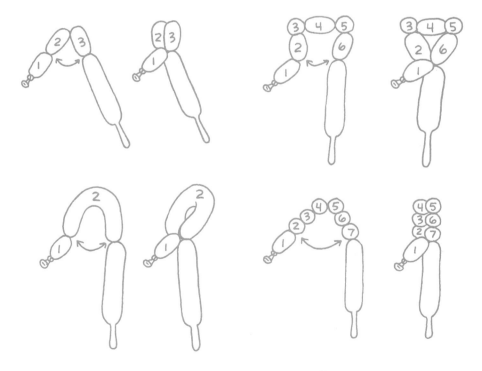

Below are examples of lock twists used to tie two balloons together.

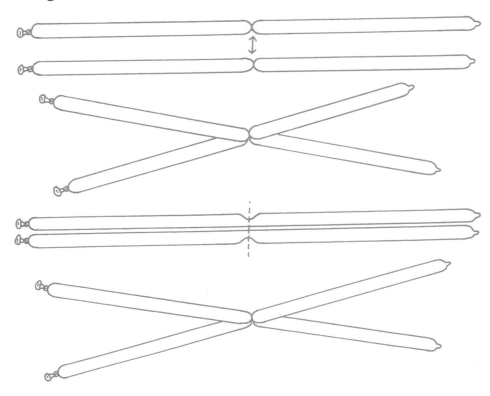

By now you may have already discovered designs revealing themselves in the bubbles that you have twisted and locked while experimenting with your balloon.

Balloon Sculpting is a lot like cloud gazing. The bubbles in a balloon, like the shapes of a floating cloud, unlock distinct images in our imaginations. Keep this in mind as you learn new designs. Use your imagination to see other design possibilities for the shapes that are created throughout this book. Sculpt balloons with your own ideas and you will become an official, card-carrying balloon artist.

Get prepared to learn and be creative. We have a whole calendar of holidays waiting to inspire us as balloon artists. So grab your pump and balloons and get ready to twist!

Chapter Two

The year begins January 1 with a New Year's celebration. The moment the clock strikes midnight, everyone is in the midst of merriment. Bells, whistles, streamers, confetti, party hats, and balloons are all in order.

For the most outrageous party hats, get out your balloons. A balloon hat is big, showy, and often has a life of its own. Fill a room with people wearing balloon hats and you have an instant party atmosphere. The best part about balloon hats is that they do not need to have specific shapes to be fun; they just need to be wearable, and that can be accomplished with one twist.

BASIC HEADBAND

Inflate a 260 until it is nearly full, then tie your knot. Wrap the balloon around the wearer's head to get a perfect fit, then lock the balloon at that point to create a loop as shown.

You have made a basic headband!

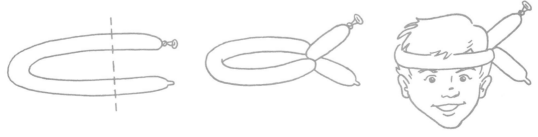

Make some minor adjustments to the headband, and you will have a more versatile cap that can become several hats in one.

Inflate a 260 leaving one to two inches of tail. Tie the knot.

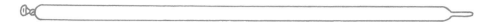

Measure the wearer's head and make a loop, locking in place as shown.

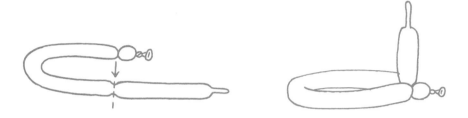

Because there is some tail left over, you now have the option of placing a pom-pom on the end of the tail. Do this by first weakening the tip of the tail: Grasp the tail with one hand and snap just the very tip by stretching and quickly releasing with the thumb and forefinger of the other hand. This will weaken the latex in the tip of the tail where the pom-pom will be.

Once you have weakened the tip, use your hand to snugly surround the entire tail, leaving only the weakened tip exposed. Do this as you squeeze the air from the last bubble up into the weakened tip, restricting the air from expanding into any other portion of the tail.

It is also necessary to grasp as much of the bubble that you are squeezing the air from for this procedure to work. You will find that if you do not, the air will just skwoosh around in the bubble and not expand into the tip of the tail.

The hat with the freshly squeezed pom-pom will look like this. The size of the pom-pom will depend on how much air you squeezed into it.

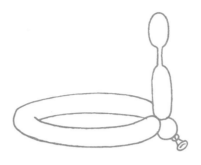

BASIC HATS

The following are some suggestions for being creative with this simple, yet versatile, hat.

BASIC HELMET

Take this hat one step further to create a helmet which will be a useful base to build countless unusual hats on.

Fully inflate a 260. Remember to burp the balloon, then tie the knot.

Create the loop for around the head as shown previously, making sure to measure the wearer. Bring the remaining portion of the balloon over the top of the loop creating an arch, and connect with a twist as shown. This will complete the basic helmet.

Make the helmet with a pom-pom by inflating a 260, leaving a

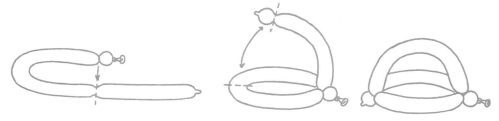

one to two inch tail. Complete the helmet in the same manner, then squeeze the pom-pom into the tip for that extra flair.

Add balloons to these basic hats, and watch them come alive.

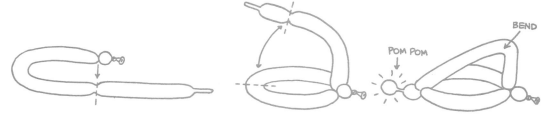

The following are some fun suggestions. What can you add? As your balloon twisting skills grow, so will your ideas for wild hats. So have fun and keep a creative, open mind to put those hats on!

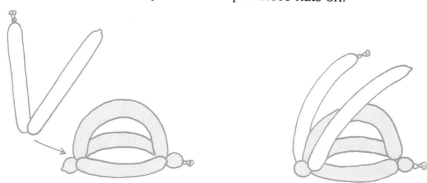

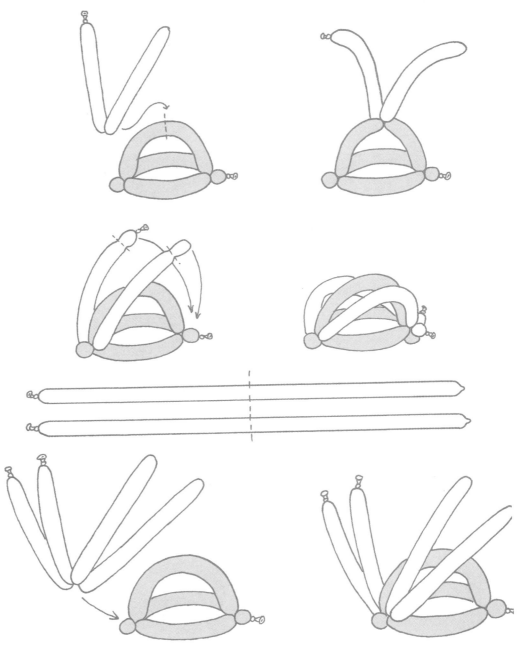

Throughout this book I will show new hats that incorporate ideas taken from other holiday designs. Balloon hats are great for any occasion, and because they are always prominently displayed (usually on someone's head), they are a great way to draw attention to yourself as a balloon artist. The more creative the hats, the more attention the wearer—and you, the balloon twister—will receive.

Making balloon hats and creating new designs will not only liven up your new year, it will keep you busy during the long, cold month of January.

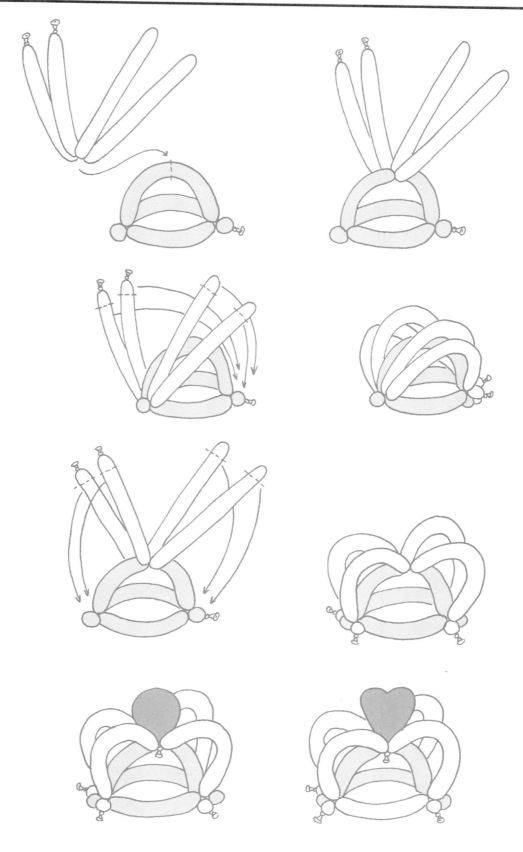

DOVE OF PEACE

Later in the month, we stop to reflect on the tremendous impact of Dr. Martin Luther King Jr. and what his life meant to peace, harmony, and brotherhood in America and the world. To honor his achievements, we can take the simple hat band and add an extra twist to convert it into a Dove of Peace as shown.

Inflate a 260 leaving two to three inches of tail. Tie a knot, and then complete as shown.

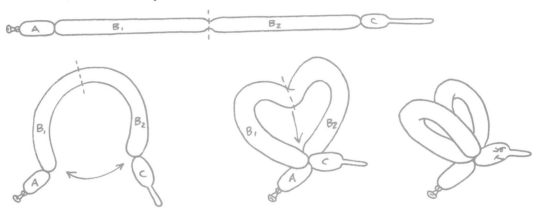

You can also add a balloon to make this a high-flying bird, or add it to a hat.

Markings on the balloon can make it appear more birdlike (or if you wish more beelike).

The best tool for marking a balloon is a felt-tipped permanent marker. Water-based markers will not work on the latex surface of a balloon. Permanent markers come in assorted colors and tip widths and are sold everywhere. Experiment with different brands to find one that you are most comfortable with.

Chapter Three

February

Two days into February we are faced with Groundhog Day, when we allow the arrival of the spring season to be predicted by a cantankerous animal who is afraid of his own shadow. If only the groundhog were a balloon animal. His translucent skin would cast a shadow of shimmering color that even the most fearful rodent would have to inspect and be mesmerized by. Spring would be here before we knew it!

Thankfully, balloon animals do exist right at our fingertips. All it takes to bring them alive is a little skill and imagination.

THE BASIC DOG

The most basic balloon animal, usually referred to as a "dog," is quite simple to make.

Inflate a 260, leaving about three to four inches of tail, and tie the knot. Create a chain that consists of three bubbles all about three inches long and lock twist the first and last joints together to create the head and ears of the dog.

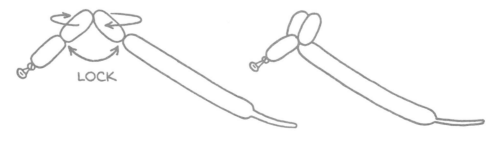

LOCK

Make three more bubbles about the same size as the last three, and lock twist in the same manner as shown. You have made the neck and front legs of the dog.

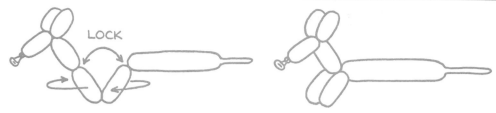

Finally, make another chain. This time, make the first bubble about four to five inches long. The second and third bubble will again be about three inches long. Lock together as shown. You have made the body and rear legs of the dog. The remaining portion of the balloon is the dog's tail.

If you have any tail left on your balloon, you can add a pompom to make a cute poodle.

BALLOON COUSINS

Experiment with different sizes of bubbles. By changing only the sizes of the bubbles and their proportions to each other, you can turn the basic animal into several different animals.

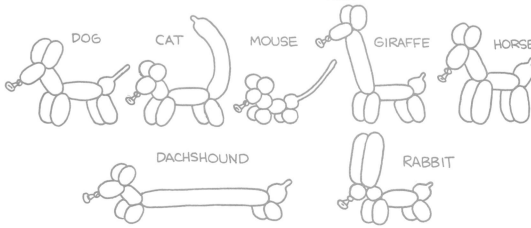

GROUNDHOG/TEDDY

Many new balloon artists are quite happy to pass the basic balloon dog off as any animal, even a groundhog. It does have a head, two ears, four legs, body and tail, after all. This idea is often used by entertainers that work with balloons and can even lead to a few laughs.

The true balloon artist, however, will be compelled to make the balloon creation look as much like the intended subject as possible. The following Groundhog design is derived from the very popular Teddy Bear design. The head of the design is also useful for kittens, squirrels, koalas, and, with some alteration, pigs. It is an excellent example of looking at a cluster of bubbles and finding multiple applications.

Needless to say, the Teddy Bear is an integral part of any serious balloon artist's repertoire. It is a design that requires some patience and practice to learn, but it will reward you with oohs and aahs from friends and audiences.

The Teddy Bear requires a new type of twist known as the "ear" twist because it resembles a small ear when completed. It is, in fact, used as the ear for this design, but has many important applications in other designs because of its unique ability to create right angles in balloons.

The ear twist is made of a small (one to two inch) bubble that is twisted so that its two joints lock together. Do this by pulling the bubble so its joints come close together, then twist about three to four times to lock. It is very much like a small fold twist, but it is necessary for the joints to be present for the ear twist to lock.

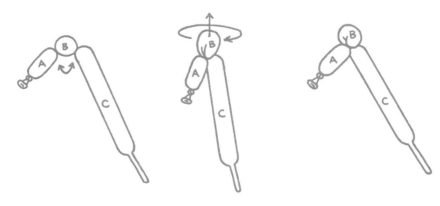

The Teddy Bear's head uses a lot of bubbles. You will make seven bubbles before you make your first lock twist, so remember to hold on to the first and last bubble of the chain until they are locked. Because so many bubbles are used in designs that use this head, leave about five to six inches of tail when you inflate the balloon.

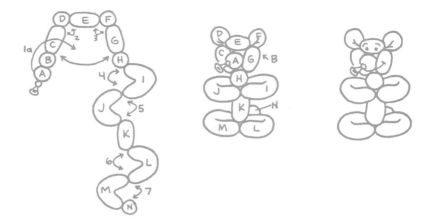

As with the basic animal, work with one chain at a time until each is locked, then begin with the bubbles of the next chain.

With some simple changes to the body of the Teddy Bear, we can make a Groundhog, poking his head out of his hole to give his weather report.

As I mentioned earlier, the Teddy Bear is quite versatile; it can be used to create other animals, or it can be added to other designs to embellish them with cuteness. The following are a few ideas courtesy of Mr. Groundhog.

Cat

Squirrel

HEARTS

Valentine's Day on February fourteenth would be nothing without the shape of love, the heart. Fortunately balloons are made in at least two sizes of ready-made heart shapes, most commonly six and nine inches after inflation. Balloon artists usually use the six-inch variety because these integrate nicely with the 260. However, the 260 itself can be made into an impressive heart shape.

Inflate a 260 fully, and tie the knot. Create a large loop by locking or tying the ends of the balloon together.

Once you have made the loop, find the top and pull it down to the bottom of the loop. Grasp the folded portion of the balloon with both hands, and gently squeeze out all of the air, holding it for a moment allowing the warmth of your hands to help form the shape. Slowly release the balloon, making sure that it does not pop out of your hands. The loop is now transformed into the outline of a heart shape.

This technique requires some practice to get beautiful heart shapes. Do not be discouraged if yours is not perfect the first time. Stay with it until you are happy with the results.

ROMANTIC HATS (AND ANIMALS WITH HEARTS)

Add bears or puppies to the heart to jazz it up, or dress up a hat with a heart or hearts.

HEART WAND

One of my most popular designs incorporates a 260 heart, a six-inch heart, and a Teddy Bear. It is the Heart Wand shown below.

Inflate a 260 leaving about one inch of tail and tie the knot.

The heart shape that you have made in the 260 should be large enough for you to insert an inflated six-inch heart as shown. Use the knotted end of the heart balloon to secure it in the base of the 260 heart. Add a Teddy Bear, and your Valentine will love you!

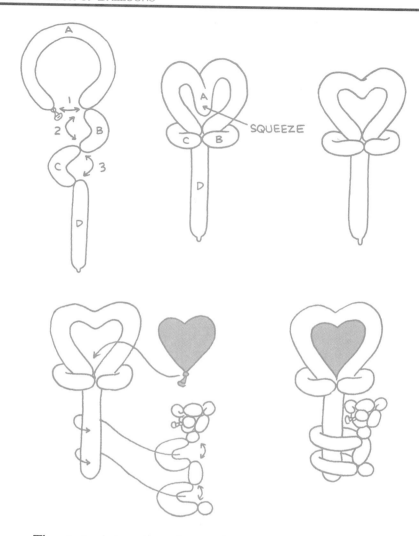

The six-inch heart can be used with other designs almost as readily as the Teddy Bear. Here are a couple of ideas:

Chapter Four

March is a blustery month. "In like a lion and out like a lamb," as people say. High winds and balloons have never really gotten along, so remember this when you make balloon designs on windy days. Hold on to those balloons, and make sure balloon hats fit tightly.

Saint Patrick's Day dresses March nicely in green. Leprechauns and shamrocks abound. The luckiest of all will find the four-leaf clover, made of balloons, of course.

SHAMROCKS

This giant four-leaf clover is made of one 260 and four, six-inch heart-shaped balloons. All of the balloons should be green (what else?). Heart balloons, usually found in red, white, or pink, also come in assorted colors and can even be bought in bags of like colors, like 260's. If you are planning on using balloons for a holiday that has specific colors you may wish to buy balloons in this manner. Consult your balloon dealer or the suppliers listed in this book for prices and availability.

Inflate two green heart balloons and tie them together at the base. Repeat this step with the remaining two heart balloons. Lock the bases of both assemblies by twisting all the knots together.

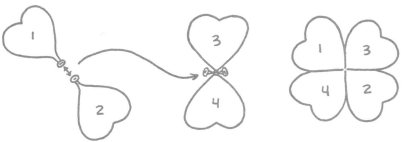

Assemble the 260 stem as shown, and add to the leaves of the clover. Three-leaf clovers, which are not as lucky but are just as fun, use three hearts tied together at the base, and are added to the stem in the same manner.

FLOWERS AND HATS

Don't be afraid to attach the clover to a hat.

Four-leaf clovers can be converted easily into tremendous flowers just by changing the colors of the leaves to convert them to petals.

Chapter Five

EASTER BUNNIES

April usually means that the Easter Bunny is nearby with his basket full of Easter eggs. This happy-go-lucky rabbit makes for a great balloon design. We have seen that it is quite easy to transform the basic balloon animal into a rabbit by making the ears longer and everything else smaller. To have him sit, make his back legs longer and tuck his front legs between them as shown.

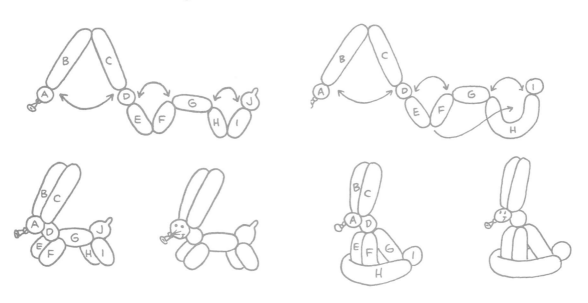

These rabbits are very cute but lack the impact of the four-balloon bunny you are about to learn. The Easter Bunny is based on my large cartoon designs that use a technique called a roll-through to make the bodies of larger characters. A roll-through is made by making two long bubbles and locking them in place as you would legs or ears on a basic balloon animal. The next bubble made will be the same length as the two locked bubbles and will be folded back to lay in the crease formed by those two bubbles.

Press the new bubble through the crease, rolling the other two bubbles to help force it through. The joints will be locked together at both ends of this roll-through formation.

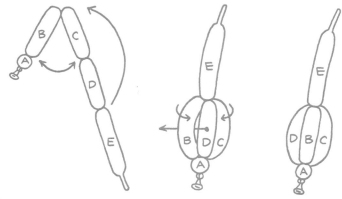

Now that you have a basic understanding of the roll-through technique, we can begin with our Easter Bunny. Start with four 260's, preferably of the same color.

BALLOON 1 (THE HEAD AND BODY)

Inflate the first balloon leaving about four to five inches of tail, and tie the knot. Follow the diagram below, using the roll-through for the body.

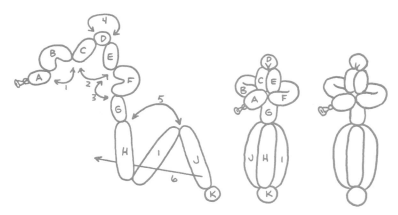

BALLOON 2 (THE ARMS)

Inflate the balloon leaving about one inch of tail. Tie the knot and complete the Bunny's arms as shown.

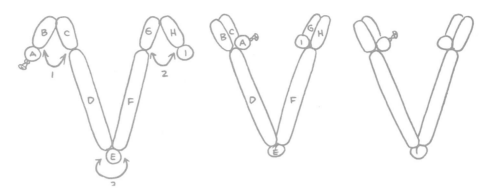

BALLOON 3 (THE LEGS)

Inflate the balloon leaving about one inch of tail. Tie the knot, and complete the legs as shown.

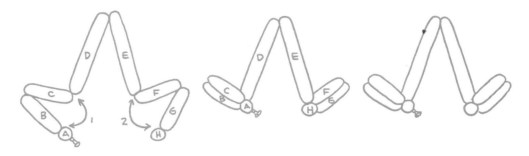

BALLOON 4 (THE EARS)

Inflate the last balloon leaving about a half an inch of tail. Tie the ends of the balloon together making a loop, and complete the ears as shown.

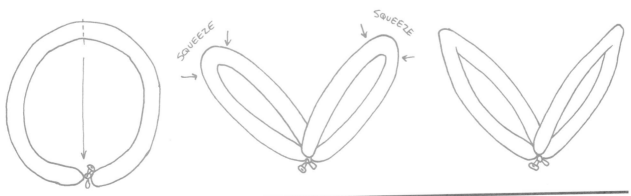

Attach the ears, arms, and legs to the body as shown. Add markings and you have one very "hoppy" Easter Bunny.

BUNNY-EARED HAT

Bunny ears can be very neatly attached to a hat to transform the wearer into a life-sized rabbit. Just add carrots.

EASTER BASKET

Use the roll-through to make an Easter Basket as shown. Take a nine-inch round balloon with a decorative print on it, or add your own markings. Inflate the balloon so that it fits snugly in the basket. Why not attach a small bunny to it, or attach the basket to the hand of the large Easter Bunny for a beautiful display piece?

Chapter Six

May flowers and Mother's Day sure go great together! We've already touched on some beautiful flowers and some heart designs that would make any Mom blush, but there can never be too much for dear ol' Mom. So here are a few more fun designs for her.

SIX-PETAL FLOWER

Our last flower design relied heavily on the use of heart balloons to create the petals, but it is possible to make a delightful flower out of 260's. The following design is a six-petal flower that resembles a daisy. It is made of two 260's.

BALLOON 1 (THE PETALS)

Inflate a 260 leaving about a half an inch of tail. Release a large amount of air so that the balloon is very relaxed, but not so much that the tail changes. Tie the ends of the balloon together to form a loop. Find the top of the loop and twist so that the loop is now in two halves.

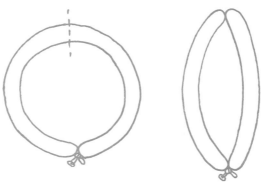

Hold both halves together, and divide them into three equal sections using a pinch twist as shown. Squeeze the balloon like an accordion so that the joints come together, and twist them so they lock in place. Arrange the newly formed petals so they rest evenly.

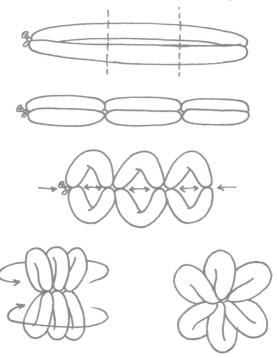

BALLOON 2 (THE STEM)

Inflate a 260 (preferably green), leaving about three inches of tail. Tie the knot and complete as shown.

Add a pom-pom to the end of the second balloon, and attach the completed first balloon to it.

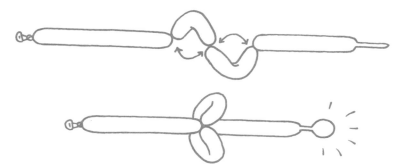

FLOWER HATS

The petal formation shown here can also be used on hats in the same manner as the heart cluster petals.

HEART CORSAGE

A nice heart design that can be worn on Mom's wrist is a heart corsage. It is made of one six-inch heart and one 260.

Inflate the 260 so that the body of the balloon is about ten to twelve inches long, with a long tail remaining. Tie the knot. Make three fold twists, beginning with the knot and ending with the base of the tail as shown. Take the tip of the tail and wrap it into the base of the three petals you have made. This will create a loop that will be used for a wristband.

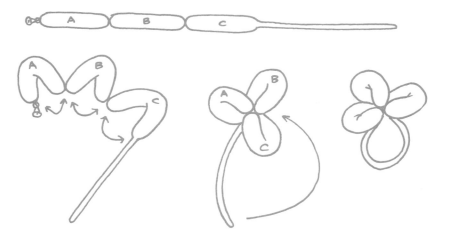

Inflate the heart balloon fully and tie the knot. Wrap the nozzle of the heart into the base of the petals. Arrange the heart so it stands upright.

You may wish to write on the heart with your permanent marker. Little notes like "I Love Mom" or "World's Greatest Mom" can make your design more personal. Slide this balloon on Mom's wrist and check for smiles.

Chapter Seven

June provides equal time for Dad as Father's Day rolls around. Dad's favorite pastimes are a good resource for fatherly balloon subject matter, with two of the most popular hobbies for dads being golf and fishing.

GOLF CLUB AND BALL

A balloon golf club and ball may not make it onto too many greens, but it will be a sure shot to Dad's heart.

Take a white round balloon, or cut about three inches off the tip of a white 260. Inflate the round balloon or the 260 tip to a size that approximates a golf ball and tie a knot.

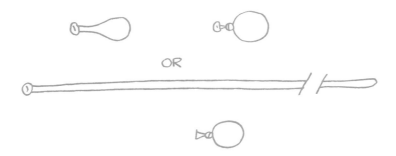

Inflate a 260 fully and tie the knot. Make a small bubble and a fold twist, and your club is done. Make a number of these, and put them in Dad's golf bag (his caddy will appreciate it).

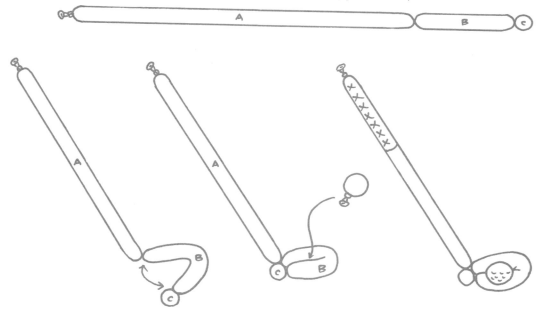

Attach the ball to the base of the club as shown.

ROD, REEL, AND DAD'S CATCH OF THE DAY

The fishing pole requires a new type of balloon and a new twist. The balloon is the *Bee Body*, also called the *321*. These balloons are made up of two colors, a light color for the body and a dark color for the tail or "stinger." The tail is generally not meant to be inflated.

Below is an illustration of what the 321 looks like when inflated.

This balloon can be made to look like a piece of fruit with a technique known as the apple twist (referred to as the tulip twist when used on 260's).

To make this twist, inflate a 321 almost to the dark part of the balloon. Tie the knot. With the index finger of one hand press the knot into the body of the balloon so that it reaches down into the tail, squeeze the tail with your other hand, grasping the knot inside, and twist several times. Remove your finger and depress the knot and tail back into the balloon slightly, allowing for a stem-like portion to remain visible. Red 321's look very much like apples, hence the apple-twist name.

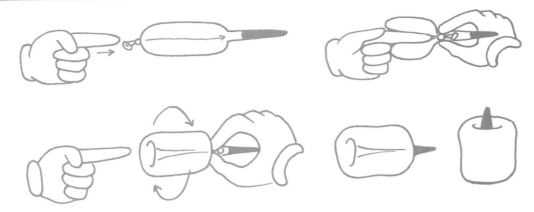

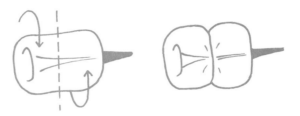

Once you have made this, find the middle of the "apple" and make a pinch twist. The tension inside the balloon will prevent it from untwisting. Set it aside. This is your fishing reel.

Now, it's time to make the fishing rod. Inflate a 260 leaving about seven to eight inches of tail. Tie the knot. Squeeze the 321 reel assembly about one-third of the way up this balloon. You now have a rod and reel with some fishing line on the end.

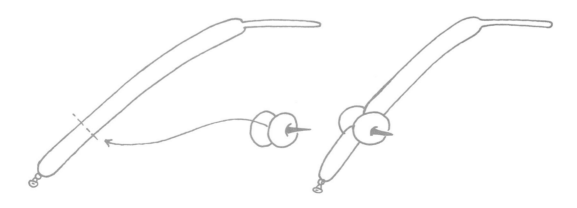

Make a fish by inflating a 260 fully and tying the knot. Fold the balloon in half and twist. On each side of that twist, make an ear twist as shown (C and D). This is the fish's mouth. Complete the fish as shown, then attach to the line by wrapping the tip around the mouth of the fish, letting the line come out from between the fish's lips.

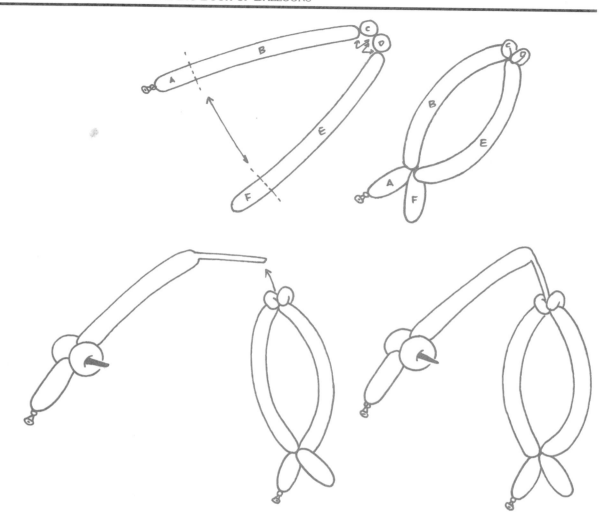

When was the last time Dad caught a blowfish on Father's Day?

Chapter Eight

So far, I have missed all of the patriotic holidays. My apologies to President's Day, Flag Day, and Memorial Day, but I've been saving my red, white, and blue designs for the granddaddy of all patriotic holidays—Independence Day, the Fourth of July.

I noted earlier that it was a good idea to buy balloons in bags of solid colors for color-specific holidays. Well, this is one of them. Almost any design you make will work on this and other patriotic days if it is red, white, and blue. Hats in these colors are a great way to celebrate America.

PATRIOTIC BRAID

A three-balloon braid of these colors is dramatic looking and quite versatile.

Inflate three 260's, one of each color, leaving very little tail. Lock them together at the bottom as shown. We will call them Balloons A, B, and C.

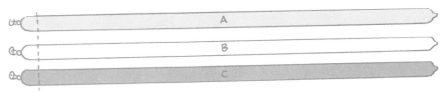

Balloon A will cross over balloon B and remain between B and C.

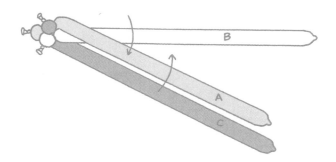

C will cross back over A and remain between B and A.
B will cross over C and remain between C and A.

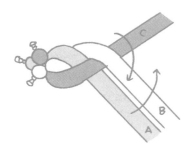

Continue braiding in this order until you reach the end, then lock twist the ends together.

Hearts, or round balloons with faces or patriotic prints, can be attached to the top of the braid for a dashing effect, and bears or other animals can be attached as well.

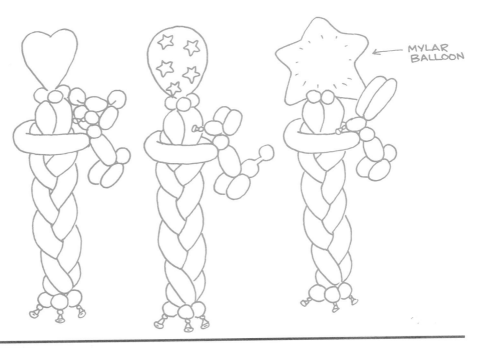

MYLAR BALLOON

YANKEE DOODLE HAT

To make a hat out of the braid, simply measure the wearer's head to determine where to stop braiding and to lock the ends together.

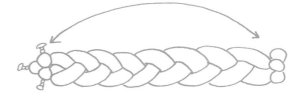

Add two more red, white, or blue 260's in the manner shown, and your hat becomes instant fireworks!

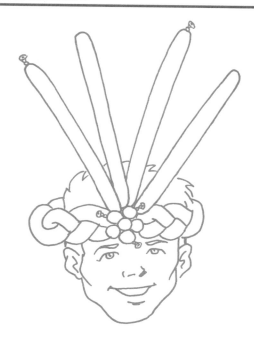

BALLOON BURST

Balloon Bursts, not to be confused with bursting balloons, look as much like fireworks exploding in the sky as anything could. With this design, all colors are acceptable, even on the Fourth of July.

Inflate eight or more 260's fully and tie their knots. Hold them together at their centers and twist. BOOM! One spectacular Balloon Burst! Without the real sound effects, of course!

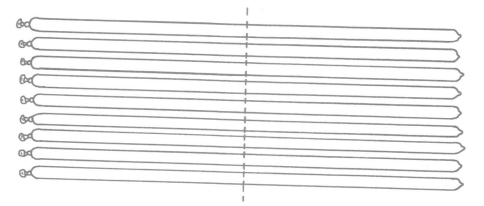

For more fun, attach the burst to a hat or a braid.

Make a bunch of Balloon Bursts and have kids jump all over them. It will sound just like fireworks and be as much fun as popping bubble wrap. Remember to clean up the mess afterwards.

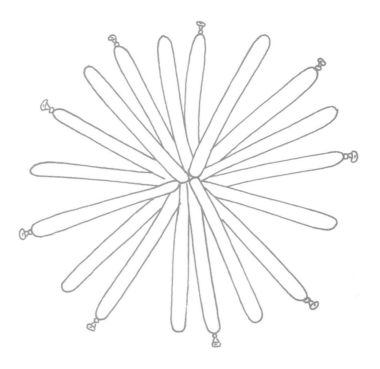

Chapter Nine

August is a great time of year if you love the summer heat and enjoy vacationing at the beach. Balloons definitely consider this time of year the "dog days" because their two worst enemies, light and heat, are bountiful. If you are planning to twist balloons at this time of year, try to keep them stored in a cool dark spot like a cooler or an insulated bag.

Unfortunately, outside, your balloon creations will be at the mercy of the atmosphere. Their lives will be short, bursting after a while from exposure to the heat, not to mention hazards like sharp blades of grass. The *best* you can hope for is oxidation, or balloon "rust," in which case your balloon will develop a hazy kind of film, and lose the brilliance of its original color and shine.

My advice is to head for the air-conditioning, if you can. Many of us who work as entertainers, however, are often forced to work outside, entertaining at picnics, fairs, and parties. We must just grin and bear it, hoping that our audiences remember our artistry and how beautiful the creations were, and not the dilapidated balloons they are left with.

Please note that balloons made inside will still be subject to the perils of heat and sun when you take them outside. In fact, the cooler air you put in the balloons inside will expand as it warms outside, making the balloons more fragile. Likewise, a balloon going into cool air from hot air is likely to shrink, for opposite reasons. As the tension in the balloon relaxes, your beautiful design tends to come undone.

RAINBOW

One design that always impresses audiences, and is a quick reminder of beautiful summer skies, is the Rainbow. This design is large and colorful, and you will enjoy making it.

The base of the Rainbow is a three-balloon braid made of white balloons. This will represent clouds. Follow the directions from our Fourth of July braid (see page 43).

Inflate a red, yellow, and blue 260 and tie their knots. Tuck each balloon's knotted end into the folds in one end of the braid, and the tail end of each balloon into the other end of the white braid, as shown.

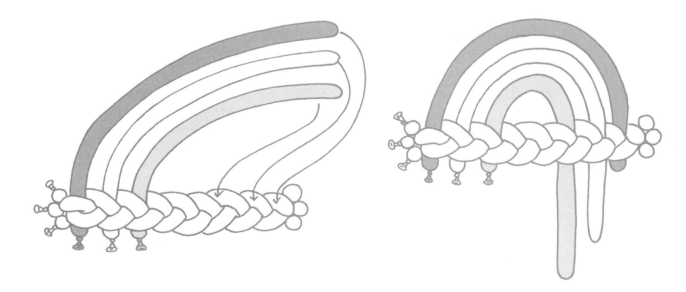

The yellow and blue balloons will extend past the braid because their arcs are smaller than that of the red one. You will want to remove the excess balloon so that the design is even. Do this by first creating a "safety bubble."

Select one of the two excessively long balloons and, at the point where you wish it to end, add a three to four inch bubble—this is the safety bubble. Hold the last joint of the newly formed bubble firmly, and remove the remaining balloon by trimming it with scissors or popping with your fingernail or other sharp object. DO NOT use your teeth! Exploded bits of broken balloon could lodge in your throat and cause you to choke.

Continue to hold the end of the safety bubble closed, and with your other hand, grasp the safety bubble by the joint on the opposite end. Release the air from the bubble, and use the deflated portion to tie a knot preventing any more air from escaping your design.

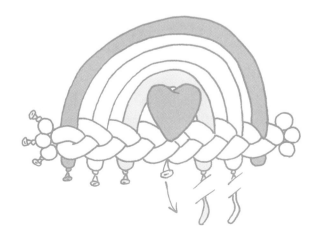

Repeat this step with the remaining long balloon. Dress up the rainbow by inflating a six-inch heart, and place it in the center of the rainbow by tucking its nozzle into a fold of the braid so that it fits tightly.

RAINBOW HAT

Make this great design into a hat by leaving the center arching balloon fully inflated and centering it so equal amounts of balloon descend beneath the braid. Lock the ends to a basic helmet as shown.

The rainbow is one of those balloons that is great all year long.

Chapter Ten

$\mathbf{S}$eptember is a time of great celebration, especially for parents, because the kids go back to school! What could be better to epitomize school days than the "Three R's": Reading, 'Riting, and 'Rithmetic.

THE BALLOON ALPHABET AND NUMBERS

It is possible to make every letter in the alphabet and every numeral with balloons using two types of twists: the ear twist helps you form right angles, and the split twist helps make almost any angle. They are illustrated below.

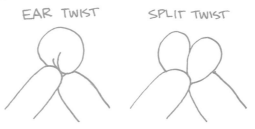

We have already seen the ear twist in the Teddy Bear in February. Below is a review of how an ear twist is formed.

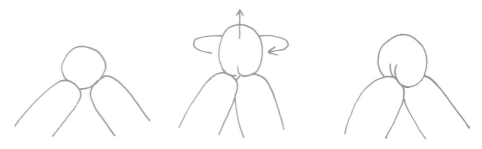

The split twist is an ear twist that is divided in half to form two smaller ear twists. It is possible to achieve the same effect by making two small ear twists. Determine which is more comfortable for you to work with.

The following diagrams describe how to make letters and numbers. You can arrange them to make words or bigger numbers by mounting them with tape, rubber cement, or cool-melt glue guns to other balloons, paper, walls, etc.

Depending on the size you wish to make your figures, you may decide to use more than one balloon. Some figures require two balloons, no matter what size they are. New balloons can be added starting at any ear or split twist. Excess balloon can be removed using the safety bubble described for the Rainbow Design in August.

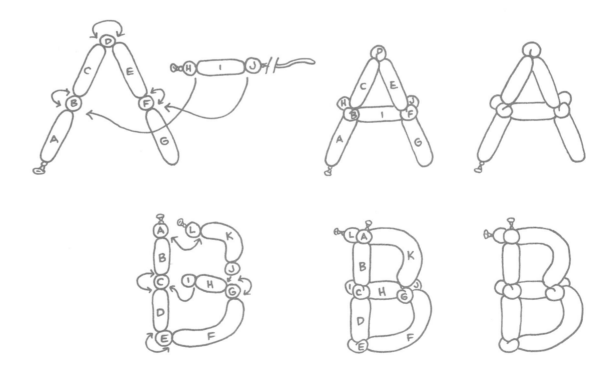

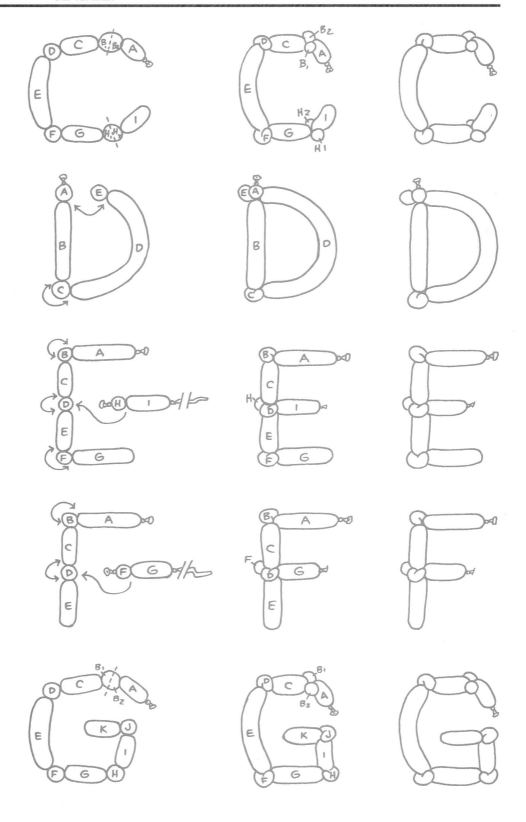

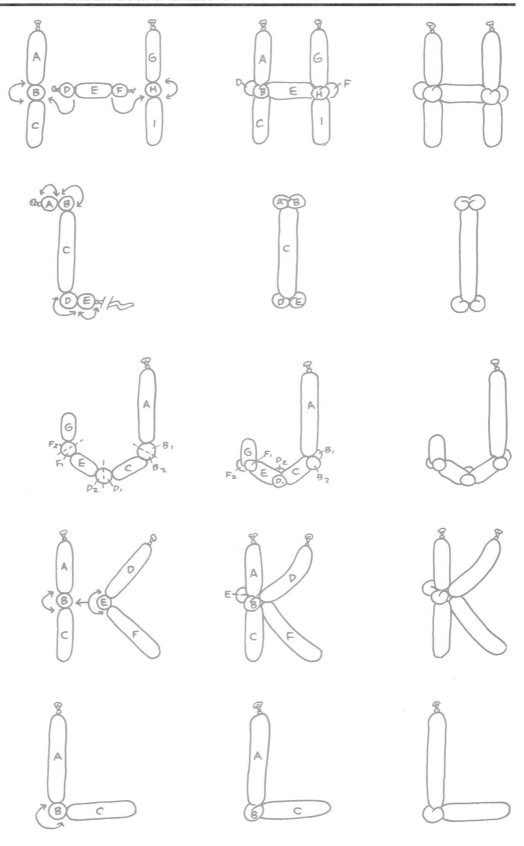

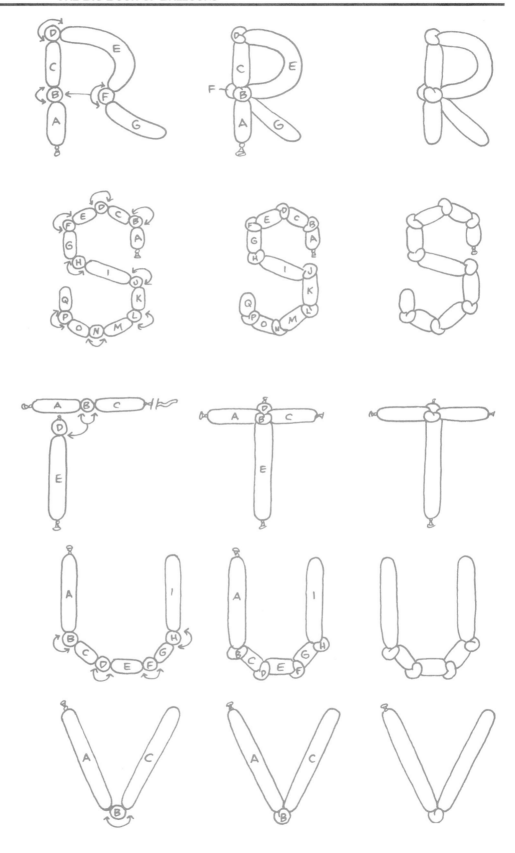

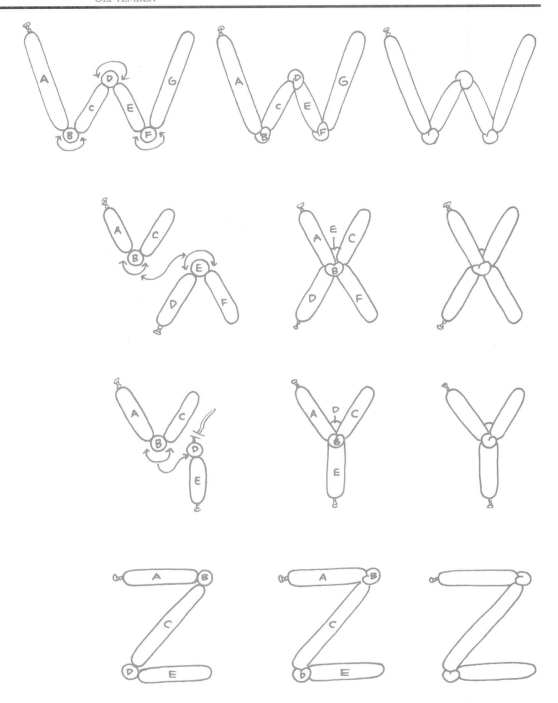

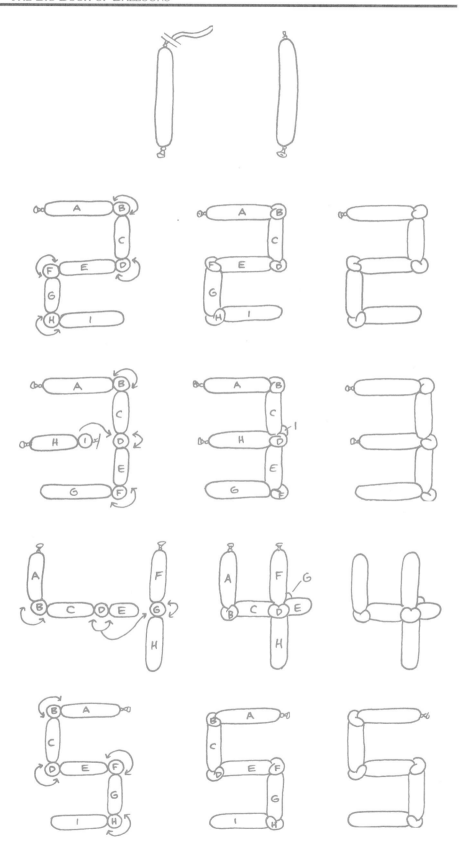

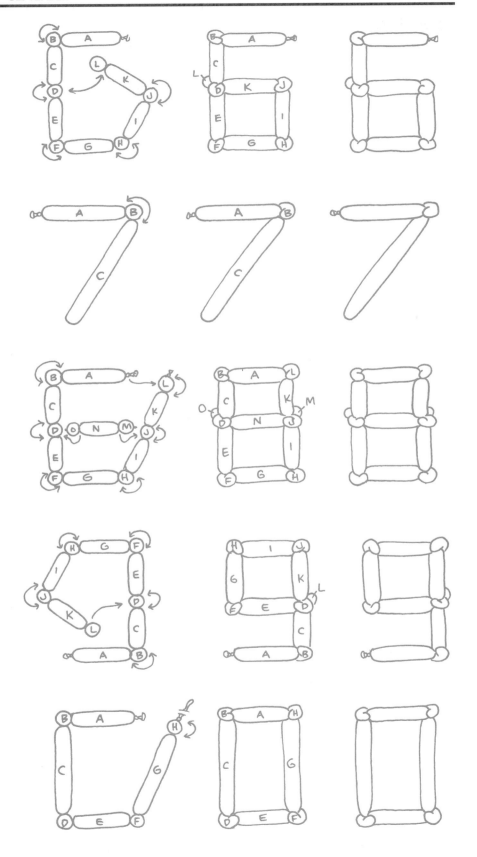

SIGN BASE

You can make a base onto which you can mount letters and numbers with the adhesives mentioned.

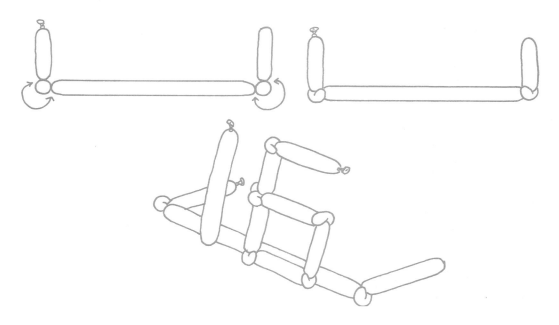

Make the base longer by adding balloons as shown.

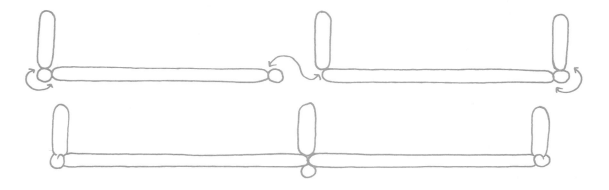

SIGN HAT

Attach a similar base to a hat for short signs or birthday numbers.

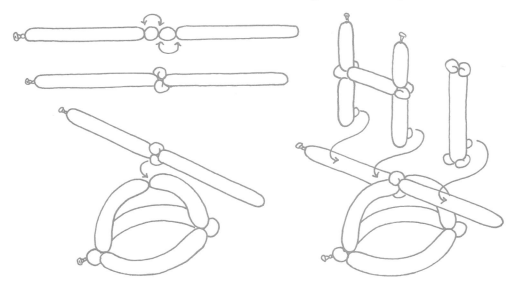

POM-POMS

Another great reason to celebrate the fall season is football. Just the mention of the word conjures thoughts of autumn aromas, brisk air, warm letterman sweaters, and school spirit.

Balloon Bursts that were described in July's pages could be made of school colors and used as giant pom-poms to rally the team.

FUN FOOTBALL HELMET

And let's not forget the team. Football helmets in team colors are a great way to support your favorite school or professional team.

They are made of three 260's, in team colors, naturally.

BALLOON 1

Construct a basic helmet as shown.

BALLOON 2

Inflate this balloon leaving about a half-inch tail. Divide the balloon in half, and attach it to the basic helmet as shown.

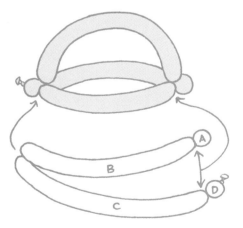
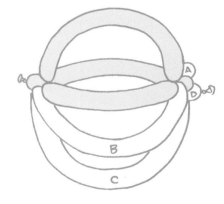

BALLOON 3

Inflate the last balloon leaving about three to four inches of tail. Tie the knot, and attach it to each bubble of the design by locking it in to the center of each as shown. Remove any excess balloon by using the safety bubble. Huddle up!

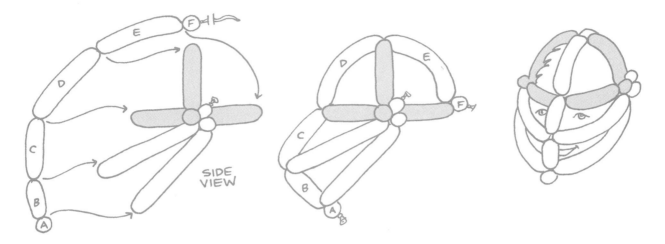

SIDE VIEW

Chapter Eleven

October

October is definitely the spookiest month of the year. Witches, goblins, skeletons, and bats seem to lurk in every corner, lit by the glow of an eerie full moon . . . BOOO!!!!!

All of these things are rather scary, but Halloween would be no fun without them!

BASIC JACK-O'-LANTERN

Our first little goblin is captured in the smiling face of a simple Jack-o'-Lantern.

Using an orange Bee Body, or 321, inflate almost to the dark part of the balloon and tie the knot. Make an apple twist as described in the June pages, and your balloon is almost instantly transformed into a pumpkin.

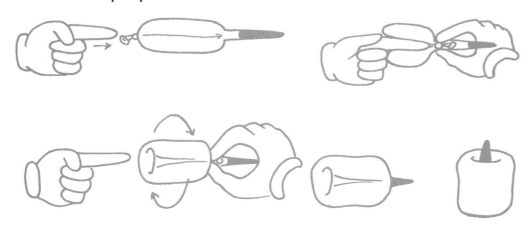

With a permanent marker, you can now add spooky faces.

JACK-O'-LANTERN HAT

Attach the pumpkin to a hat by tying the tail of an uninflated 260 to the knot of the inflated *Bee Body*. Complete the apple twist, then inflate the 260, and create a basic hat as shown.

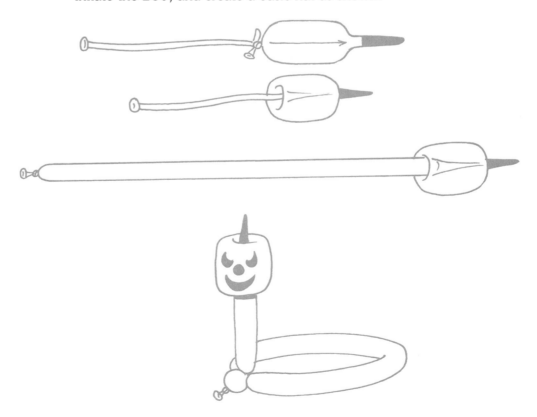

BLACK CAT ON A FULL MOON

Full moons and black cats go great together, and they make a fine balloon design. Use two 260's, one orange and one black.

BALLOON 1 ORANGE (THE MOON)

Inflate the balloon leaving about a half-inch tail. Tie the ends together forming a circle.

BALLOON 2 BLACK (THE KITTY CAT)

Inflate the balloon leaving about three inches of tail and tie the knot. Make the Cat's head the same way you would make the Teddy Bear's head (described in February's pages) and attach to the Moon as shown. Be careful to use slightly smaller bubbles when making the Cat so that its tail can be as long as possible.

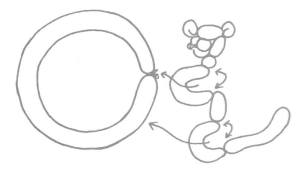

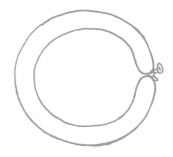

CAT AND MOON HAT

To attach this design to a hat, make the Moon using the lock twist method, and attach the top of the basic helmet to the loop at this point. Mount the Cat on the Moon in the same manner, but at a different point on the circle.

SCREECHY BAT

The Bear Head is also useful when styling a Bat out of balloons. The following Bat requires two black 260's.

BALLOON 1 (THE BAT'S BODY)

Inflate the balloon leaving about three inches of tail and tie the knot. Complete the Bat's Head and body as shown, using a Bear's Head and a roll-through for the body.

BALLOON 2 (THE BAT'S FLAPPING WINGS)

Inflate the second balloon fully, and make a loop by tying ends together. Divide the balloon in half, and attach it to the body as shown. Once the wings are attached, twist each wing to create a joint where the tip of the Bat's wings should be. Use the illustration below as a guide.

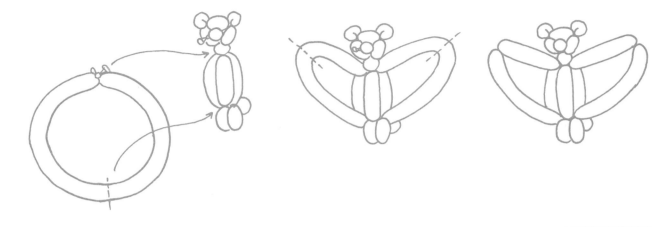

BAT ON A STICK, OR BAT HAT

Attach a fully inflated 260 to the base of the Bat to make him fly or to convert him into a hat as shown.

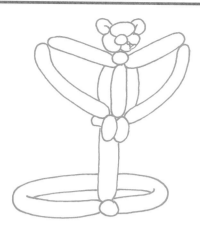

ONE-BALLOON BAT

Here is a diagram for a simple One-Balloon Bat.

Inflate a black 260 leaving about two to three inches of tail. Tie the knot and complete as shown.

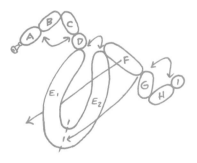
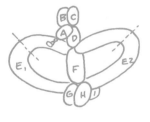

BONY SKELETON

Hang a Skeleton in your closet with the next bony design, which uses four white 260's.

BALLOON 1 (THE HEAD AND BODY)

Inflate the balloon leaving about three to four inches of tail. Tie the knot and complete the head and body as shown.

BALLOON 2 (ARMS)

Inflate the balloon leaving about three inches of tail. Tie the knot and complete the arms as shown. Attach to the body.

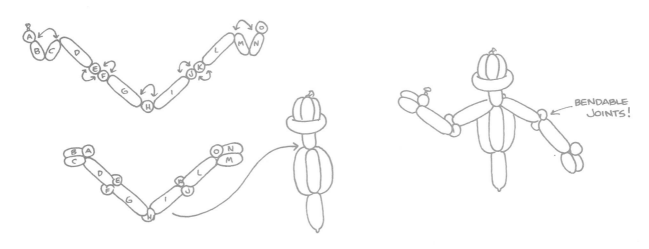

BENDABLE JOINTS!

BALLOONS 3 AND 4 (LEGS)

Inflate the balloon leaving about two inches of tail. Tie the knot and complete a leg as shown. Repeat with balloon four to complete the other leg and attach to the body as shown. Add details to the face and chest with a permanent marker.

　　　Notice that the use of split twists for the knees and elbows allows your skeleton to be posable.

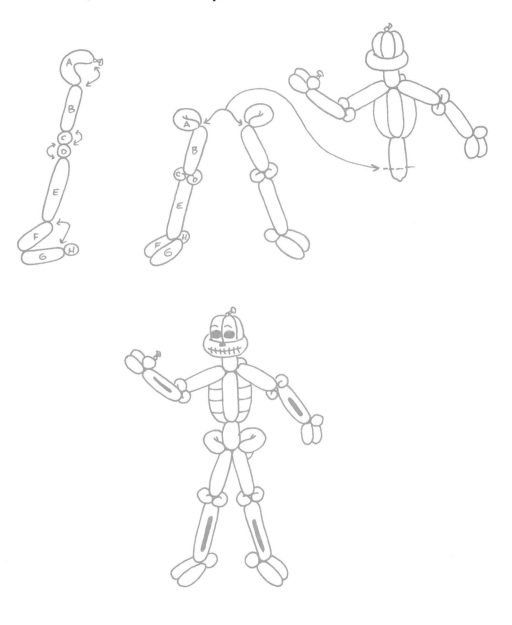

CACKLING WITCH

Witches reign as the Queens of Halloween and surely need a classy balloon design to represent them on this holiday.

This design requires five balloons: one white and three black 260's, and one green six-inch heart.

BALLOON 1: WHITE 260 (EYES)

Inflate the white 260 so the body is about four inches long. Tie the knot. Make two ear twists, starting with the knot as shown. Using the safety bubble, remove excess balloon. These are the Witch's eyes. Set them aside.

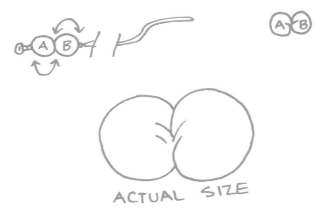

BALLOON 2: GREEN SIX-INCH HEART (HEAD)

Inflate the heart, then give it a large burp prior to tying the knot. Grasp one of the lobes of the heart and twist it, creating a two-inch bubble. Continue to hold and lock it in place using the eyes. The new bubble is the Witch's nose; the rest of the balloon is her head.

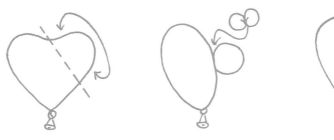

BALLOONS 3 AND 4: BLACK 260 (ARMS, LEGS, AND BODY)

Inflate the balloons leaving about two inches of tail. Tie the knot and assemble as shown. Attach to balloons 3 and 4 to complete the body, and then attach the head.

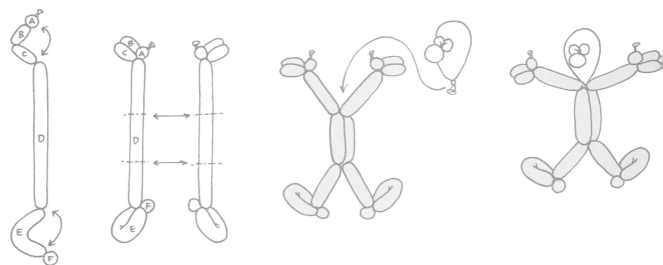

BALLOON 5: BLACK 260 (THE HAT)

Inflate the balloon leaving about a half-inch tail. Tie the knot. Measure the Witch's head, and make a basic helmet to fit her. Because her head is very small, the helmet will be quite tall. Find the top of the hat, and twist to form a joint. This will cause the helmet to come to a point like a Witch's hat. Place the balloon on her head. Finally, use a permanent marker to finish her face. Trick or Treat!

Chapter Twelve

November is the time of year that we all set aside to give thanks for our family and friends, our successes and good fortunes, and for a bountiful harvest. All of us, that is, except Tom the Turkey. For him, November is a very stressful month. Alas, if it were not for Tom's presence at the dinner table, Thanksgiving would not be the same.

Images of the turkey are everywhere this time of year, almost as a badge of honor for Tom's supreme sacrifice. The turkey, at one time, almost edged out the bald eagle as the national bird, probably because of his important role in providing sustenance to the Pilgrims and other early settlers of America. I guess the eagle got the nod since the idea of a turkey on the side of a mail truck didn't seem too appealing.

Nevertheless, the turkey gets his due on Thanksgiving, inspiring the following balloon creation.

THE TURKEY HAT

The Turkey Hat is made of three 260's—two brown and one red.

Inflate the two brown balloons leaving about a half-inch tail on each. Tie their knots and assemble as shown. This will serve as the Turkey's body and the base of the hat.

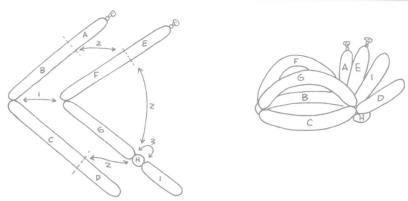

Now for Tom's head and neck. Inflate the red balloon, leaving about four to five inches of tail. Tie the knot and assemble as shown. Make the curve in the neck by pulling on the tail to begin a tight spiral, ending at the base. Rub the spiral with your hand to warm the latex to help it to hold the shape. Release the spiral, and the Turkey's neck will have an elegant curve. Attach the neck to the body as shown.

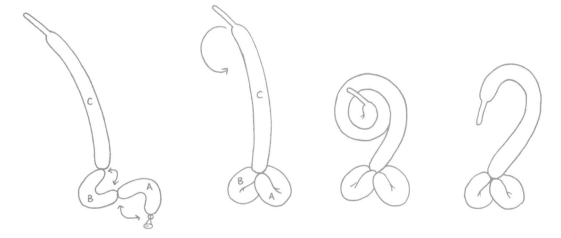

Spread the body of the Turkey over the wearer's head, and you have a great Turkey Hat!

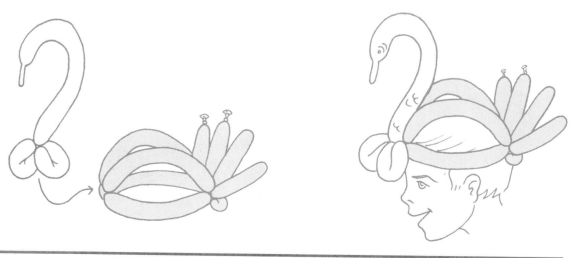

TURKEY

Transform the Turkey Hat into a complete model of a Turkey by adding feet. Inflate an orange 260, leaving about two inches of tail. Tie the knot. Assemble as shown, removing any excess balloon using the safety bubble. Attach legs to the body as shown.

THE CORNUCOPIA

Turkey is not the only food served at Thanksgiving. The entire harvest was a great tribute to the successful and nurturing friendship that developed between the Native Americans and the Pilgrims. The cornucopia, also known as the Horn of Plenty, traditionally displays a wide array of fruit and vegetables indicative of a productive harvest.

The cornucopia is a complex balloon design requiring a technique known as a "weave." It also, of course, is accompanied by an array of balloon fruits and vegetables to make it look interesting.

The cornucopia itself requires a minimum of seven 260's to form its shape. Other balloons can be added to make it larger. I prefer yellow balloons to achieve a golden look normally associated with cornucopias.

Begin with one balloon. Inflate it, leaving about five to six inches of tail. Tie the knot and assemble as shown. This will be the curled tip of the cornucopia. As balloons are added, this tip will taper out to a large opening, like the bell of a horn.

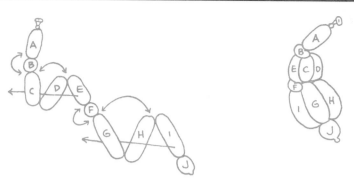

Inflate the next six balloons, leaving at least six inches of tail on each one. Make three groups of two by tying their nozzles together as shown. Cross the three pairs at the knotted joints and twist, forming a cluster like the clover shown in February's pages. Attach the first balloon at this point.

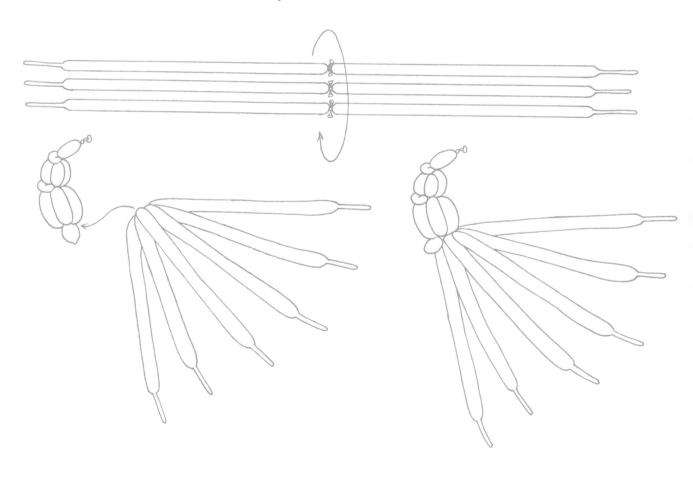

Make a two-inch bubble and an ear twist on each of the six balloons.

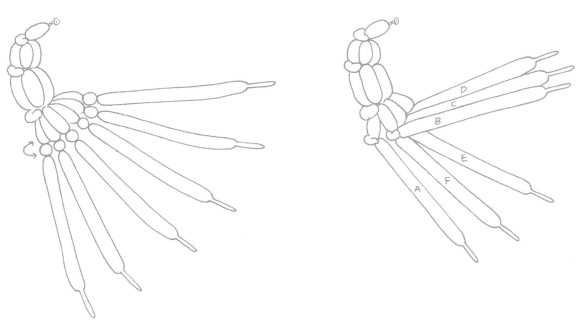

At this point, we will label the remaining portions of the balloons A,B,C,D,E, and F. Make a one-inch bubble in balloon A, and attach it to the ear twist on balloon B. Make a one-inch bubble in balloon B, and attach it to the ear twist in balloon C. Continue in this fashion until you connect balloon F with the ear twist on balloon A, completing the first cycle.

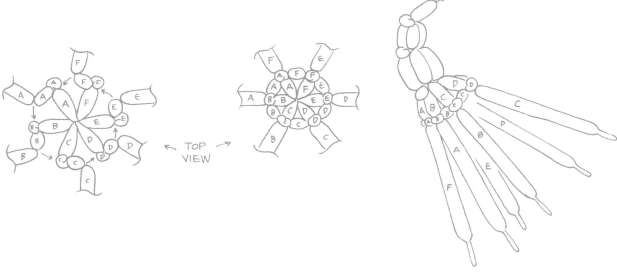

TOP VIEW

Make a three-inch bubble in balloon A, then an ear twist. Make a two-inch bubble in balloon B, then an ear twist. Make a one-inch bubble in balloon C, then an ear twist. Make a one-inch bubble in balloon D, then an ear twist. Make a two-inch bubble in balloon E, then an ear twist. Finally, make a three-inch bubble in balloon F, then an ear twist. We will call the bubbles of varying sizes "down bubbles." Their size differences are necessary to make our cornucopia curl. Make a two-inch bubble in each balloon, and connect each to the ear twist of the next, forming a circle as we did in the previous illustration. These bubbles will be called "cross bubbles."

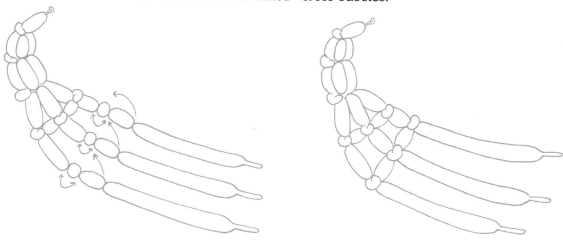

This time balloon F will be starting in the down lane where balloon A was last time, so make a three-inch bubble in balloon F, then an ear twist. Make a two-inch bubble in balloon A, then an ear twist. Make a one-inch bubble in balloon B, then an ear twist. Make a one-inch bubble in balloon C, then an ear twist. Make a two-inch bubble in balloon D, then an ear twist. Finally, make a three-inch bubble in balloon E, then an ear twist.

This time make each cross bubble three inches, and connect them to the neighboring ear twist. As you continue with each new tier of the weave, the cross bubbles will become an inch larger. This is done to make the mouth of the cornucopia gradually open wider as each tier is added.

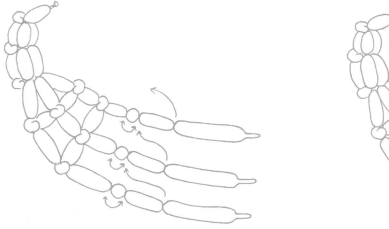
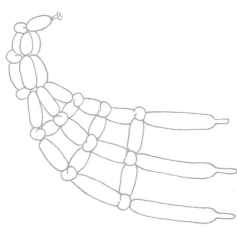

Again, make the down bubbles and ear twists in each balloon, this time starting with balloon E as a three-inch bubble, F as a two-inch bubble, A as a one-inch bubble, and so on. The cross bubbles will be four inches. Lock them to each next ear twist and complete the tier.

By now, the balloons are probably running out of tail room to work with. Use a safety bubble to remove any excess balloon from each and tie knots. Tuck the knots behind each of their respective ear twists.

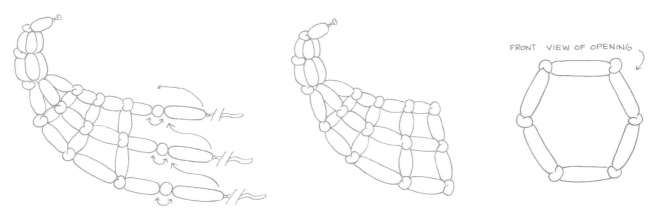

FRONT VIEW OF OPENING

At this point, you can stop and say, "Hey, I made a cornucopia!" Or you can continue to make it larger. This is entirely up to you, the balloon artist. To make the design larger, inflate six more yellow 260's, leaving an ample amount of tail in each. Tie each knot and attach to an ear twist, and continue making tiers, remembering to make the cross bubble a bit larger each time. If you're patient enough, you could make a *room-sized* cornucopia!

Note that at anytime along the way, a balloon may break. This does not mean you have to start at the very beginning. Because the ear twists are so tight, there is little chance of air escaping. So wrap what is left of the broken balloon around the ear twist it is part of. Inflate a new balloon, tie the knot, attach to that same twist, and continue with your design.

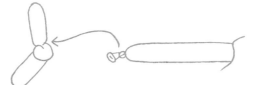

THE BOUNTIFUL HARVEST

Now that you have made the cornucopia, it is time to fill it with fruit and vegetables.

APPLES

We have already described how to make apples and pumpkins out of Bee Bodies using the apple twist. Vary the colors of the balloons for a variety of fruit. You may also vary sizes by inflating with different amounts of air.

BANANAS

Make a bunch of bananas by making a long yellow roll-through. Remove any excess balloon, and bend the bunch to give your bananas some curve.

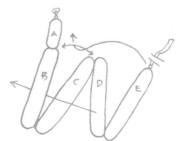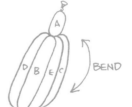

SQUASH/GOURDS

Make squash or gourds by making smaller roll-throughs starting at the knot of the balloon. After the roll-through, curl the end of the balloon and remove any excess.

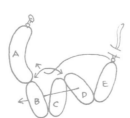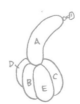

GRAPES/BERRIES

Make grapes and berries by making chains of small one-inch bubbles. Use roll-throughs and lock twists to bunch them together as shown. Because these balloons will require a lot of twisting, leave an ample amount of tail. Any excess can be removed. Change colors to add variety. Good colors are green, purple, blue, and red.

PUMPKINS/MELONS

Larger pumpkins and melons can be made using round balloons inflated to the desired size. If you wish, you can use the apple twist method on round balloons, but it is necessary to tie the inserted knot with a thin piece of string or a fragment of balloon as shown.

Pack your fruit into and out of the cornucopia, arranging as you desire. You may want to use tape, rubber cement, or a cool-melt glue gun to assist in attaching balloons to each other. Feel free to garnish your design with leaves, pipe cleaners, and nuts. Be sure that whatever you use is not sharp and will not pop the design that you've worked so hard on.

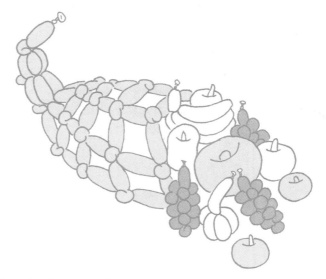

Your final Horn of Plenty will be a feast for anyone's eyes!

Chapter Thirteen

December is, above all, the month of great joy and gift giving. By now, if you have mastered most of the designs in this book, you are a gifted balloon artist. Now is not the time to celebrate, however, because there are still a lot of designs to be learned, especially with Hannukah and Christmas ahead of us.

CANDLES

Hannukah usually falls first on the calendar (sometimes as early as November). It is the Jewish celebration of lights and a commemoration of their triumph over oppression thousands of years ago. The most recognizable symbol of Hannukah is the Menorah, a lamp that burns nine candles, the tallest usually located in the center.

To make a Menorah, the lamp is made first, with the candles added later. However, for the purpose of showing how the design is made, the candles' construction are best shown first.

Each candle in the Menorah is made the same way, requiring two 260's, one white and one orange.

BALLOON 1 (THE CANDLE)

Inflate the white 260 so that the body is about eight to ten inches long and tie the knot.

BALLOON 2 (THE FLAME)

Cut about three to four inches off the tip of the orange balloon and discard the nozzle end.

Inflate the tip so that it inflates all but about a half-inch of the very tip. Release enough air so that you can tie a knot, and leave about one inch of the nozzle. After you have done this, tie another knot in the very end of the nozzle as shown in the illustration. This is known as an anchor knot.

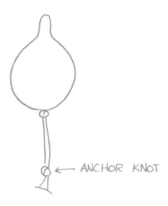

Align the anchor knot from balloon two with the knot from balloon 1. Press both knots into the body of the balloon with your index finger and make a tulip twist, locking both knots in place. This technique is also called a marriage twist, because it joins two balloons together. Be sure to press both knots in far enough so that the orange bubble is seated firmly in the tulip twist. The result is a candle with a flame. You can pull on the tip of the flame to stretch the bubble and make it appear more flamelike.

Once you have completed your candle, determine the size you wish it to be, use a safety bubble to remove any excess balloon, and tie a knot.

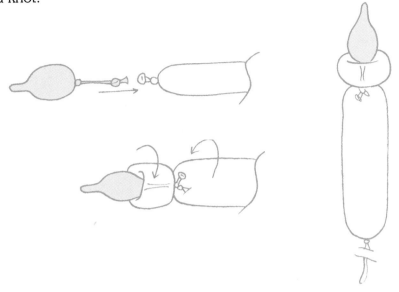

SIMPLE MENORAH

As with almost any design, there can be several different approaches to achieve a desired effect. The following are two possibilities for beautiful balloon Menorahs.

The first is the more simple of the two. It requires three 260's to make the lamp, to which you will add nine candles constructed in the manner just described. I recommend that yellow, blue or white balloons be used to make the lamp. This color choice can vary, but all three balloons should be of the same color.

BALLOON 1 (THE CENTER STEM)

Inflate a 260 leaving about five inches of tail. Tie the knot and construct as shown. Where split twists are shown, make each bubble of the split twist about one inch in size.

BALLOON 2 (ONE "BRANCH")

Inflate a 260, leaving about six inches of tail. Tie the knot and construct as shown, again making each bubble of the split twists about an inch in size.

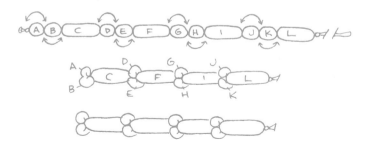

BALLOON 3 (THE OTHER "BRANCH")

Repeat the same procedure used on balloon 2. Attach balloon 2 and 3 to balloon 1 as shown.

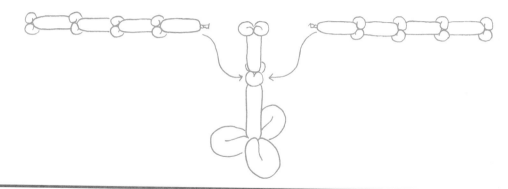

Attach candles by locking the knot at the bottom of each candle into each split twist as shown.

When finished, the Menorah should look like this.

DELUXE MENORAH

The more complicated Menorah requires seven 260's to make the lamp. Again, all of these balloons should be the same color. I prefer to use yellow.

BALLOON 1

Inflate a 260, leaving about eight inches of tail, and tie the knot. This will be the main support of the lamp. Assemble as shown, keeping in mind that each split twist should be about one inch. The bubbles that are between each split twist should be about two inches. It is important for the integrity of the structure that these bubbles be as uniform as possible.

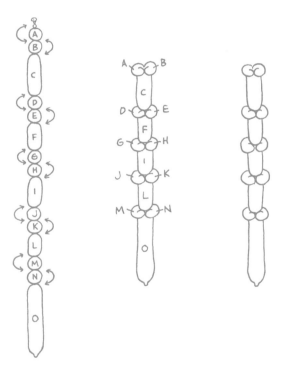

BALLOON 2

Inflate a 260, leaving about a half-inch tail. Tie the ends together to form a loop. Complete as shown, forming a base that resembles a four-petaled flower.

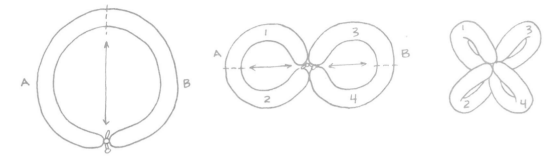

Attach the base to balloon 1 as shown.

BALLOON 3

Inflate a 260 about halfway. Tie the knot and construct as shown, using one-inch bubbles for split twists and ear twists. Attach to the main support as shown. Remove any excess balloon by using a safety bubble. This balloon will be the Menorah's innermost branches.

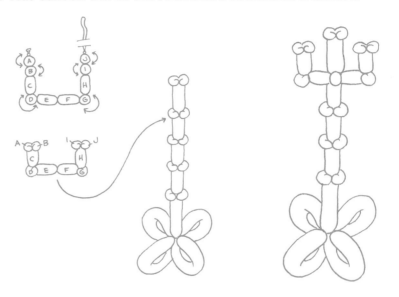

BALLOONS 4 AND 5

These balloons are assembled exactly like balloon 2, except each is a bit deeper and a bit longer. This will vary, depending on your own measurements. Try to keep the tops even and the holders evenly spaced as shown in the illustration.

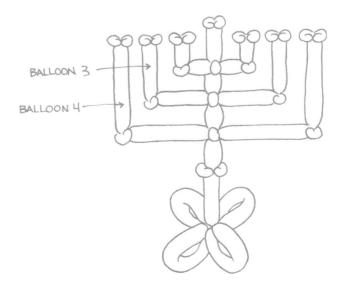

BALLOONS 6 AND 7 (THE OUTERMOST BRANCHES)

The construction of these balloons is identical. Inflate each balloon, leaving about four inches of tail, and tie the knot. Assemble as shown, removing any excess balloon by using a safety bubble. Attach each to the main support. All of the candle holders should be evenly spaced and level at the top, as shown.

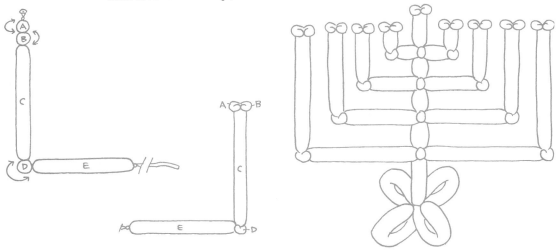

Attach candles to the lamp as shown in the previous lamp design. You may wish to make the center candle slightly taller than the rest. The final Menorah should look like the illustration below and, if made properly, will stand firmly on its base. For added support, you can mount this design on a cardboard base with two-sided tape, rubber cement, or a cool-melt glue gun.

Either Menorah looks great attached to a basic helmet.
Give it a try!

DREIDEL

Another nice balloon design for Hannukah is a Dreidel, a toplike toy that Hebrew children have played with for centuries. The Dreidel is a four-sided box shape with a point at the bottom and a post at the top for spinning the toy.

The Dreidel is created in much the same way as the cornucopia from the November chapter, using a similar weave technique that in this case will require only four balloons instead of six. One extra balloon will be added to create the post, bringing the total number of balloons used for this design to five. These balloons can all be the same color or they can be mixed. I like to make the box one color and use a different color for the post.

BALLOONS 1 TO 4

Inflate each of the four balloons about halfway. Tie the knots together in groups of two. Lock both groups together to form a cluster of four balloons, as shown.

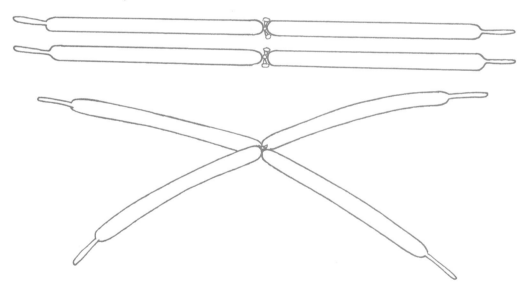

Take each balloon and make a four-inch bubble, then an ear twist as shown.

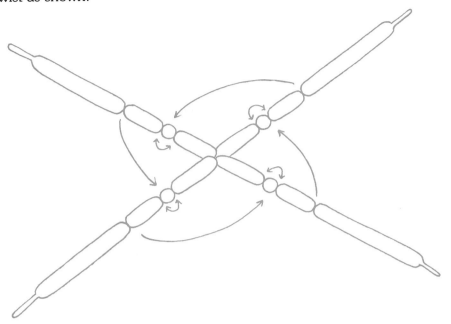

Make a four-inch bubble again in each balloon, this time locking it to the ear twist of the balloon next to it until a square shape is completed. The four original bubbles should come to a pyramidlike point.

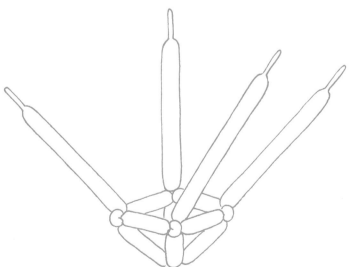

Make a five- to six-inch bubble in each balloon, and end with an ear twist. Make sure that the bubbles are all the same size.

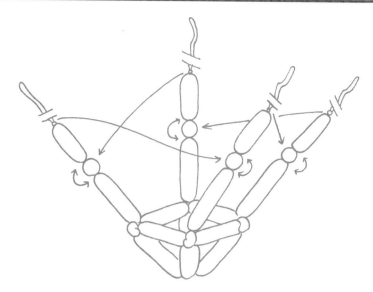

Make four-inch bubbles in each balloon connecting to the ear twist of the balloon next to it. Continue until you have finished the square shape as shown. Remove any excess from each balloon using the safety bubble.

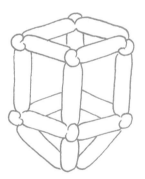

BALLOON 5 (THE POST)

Inflate the balloon fully and remember to burp it. Tie the knot. Make a one-inch bubble at the tail end of the balloon and lock into the pointed end of the box. The rest of the balloon should extend through the box and out the other end. Find a point in the balloon that is about four to five inches beyond the box and make a twist. Add a safety bubble, remove any excess balloon from this point, and tie a knot.

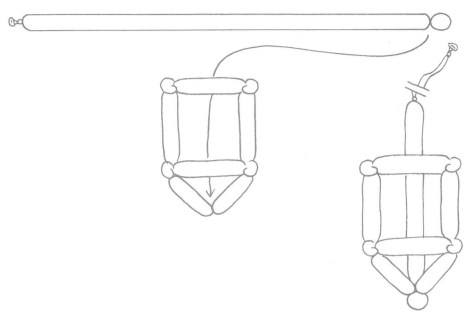

Use a permanent market to add traditional symbols to your Dreidel. The Dreidel balloon actually works like the original clay toys, but be careful to keep it away from sharp objects that could surely pop the spinning balloon.

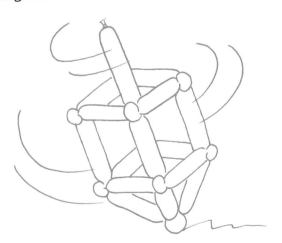

STAR OF DAVID

One last design that is great for Hannukah is the six-pointed star or the Star of David. Depending on the size you wish to make it, this Star can be made with as few as three balloons. Make the Star larger by increasing the measurement sizes, which will require extra balloons to be added. All bubbles should end with an ear twist. Any excess balloon should be removed using a safety bubble, and any balloon added should be added to the joint created by the ear twist.

Most important, every bubble in the Star that is not an ear twist should be the same length. If one bubble is four inches long, every other bubble will be four inches long. Ear twists should also be all the same size (not to exceed one inch) no matter how big the Star is.

We will construct our star using three balloons.

BALLOON 1

Inflate the balloon leaving about seven inches of tail. Tie the knot and create a hexagonal shape as shown.

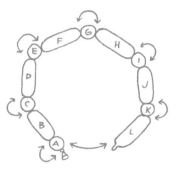 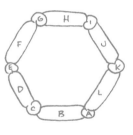

BALLOONS 2 AND 3

Inflate each balloon, leaving about seven inches of tail, and tie the knot. Create a three-point zig-zag in each as shown.

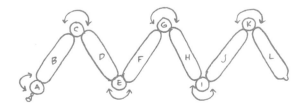 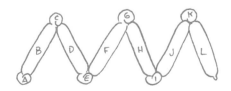

Attach the zig-zags to the hexagon as shown, using the ear twists to lock and stabilize the balloons at their joints.

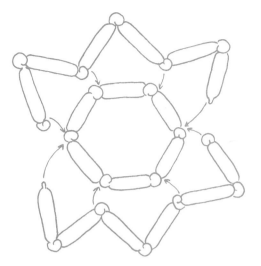 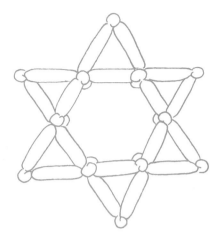

STAR HELMET

You can attach the Star to a basic helmet by locking an ear twist that forms the tip of one of the Star's points to the top of the helmet as shown.

The Star of David can be used for other Jewish holidays as well.

December is also host to one of the year's most joyous holidays, Christmas, the celebration of the birth of the Christ child. Over the centuries, so many traditions for celebrating this holiday have emerged that there are an endless number of design possibilities for balloon sculptures. Though Christmas is a religious holiday for Christians, many images are widely accepted as symbols of the holiday season which extends from Thanksgiving to New Year's.

I have selected some of the most colorful and popular symbols of the season that will put a smile on every face, especially the children's.

RUDOLPH

One of the most recently developed characters associated with Christmas who was met with instant acceptance is Rudolph the Red-nosed Reindeer. This design is chosen to lead our parade of Christmas designs because it utilizes the anchor knot and marriage twist that we have just worked with for the candles of the Menorah. Besides, Rudolph's Red Nose always leads the way!

This very basic Rudolph uses three 260's. I suggest a red, a brown, and a white one.

BALLOON 1 (THE NOSE)

Cut about three to four inches from the tip of a red 260. Inflate the tip so that it is about an inch around. Tie a knot, and then an anchor knot as shown.

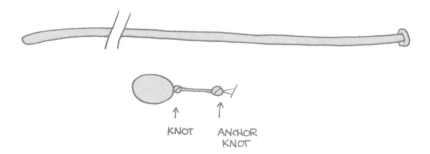

BALLOON 2 (THE BODY)

Inflate a brown 260 leaving about four inches of tail. Tie the knot. Attach balloon 1 to balloon 2 by using the marriage twist, then complete the figure of the reindeer as shown.

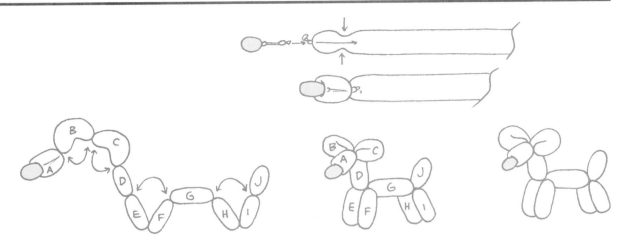

BALLOON 3 (THE ANTLERS)

Inflate a white 260, leaving about two inches of tail, and tie the knot. Assemble the antlers as shown. Attach the completed antlers to the head of Rudolph.

Of course "regular" reindeer can be made the same way, by either changing the red balloon to black, or by not adding the nose balloon at all as shown below.

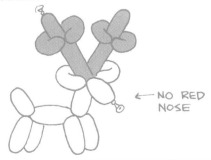

← NO RED NOSE

REINDEER HAT

Reindeer hats can be made easily by adding antlers to the top of a basic helmet. Make Rudolph hats by adding a partially inflated red round balloon.

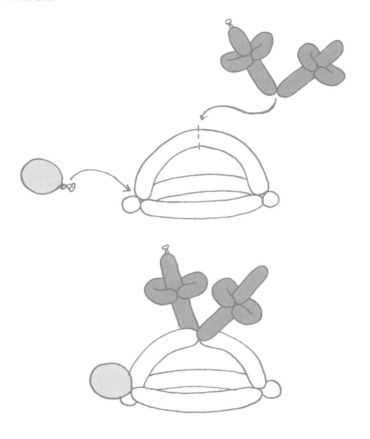

SANTA

While we are borrowing techniques from other designs, let's look back on the Witch Design from Halloween and see how we can transform that design into Santa Claus, one of the most popular heroes of children everywhere.

Our Santa balloon will require one pink six-inch heart, three red 260's, two white 260's, and one small, white, round balloon (for which you can substitute the tip of a white 260).

BALLOON 1

Inflate a white 260 about halfway. Tie the knot and construct Santa's beard and mustache as shown. Use the safety bubble to remove any excess balloon.

BALLOON 2 (SANTA'S HEAD)

Loosely inflate a pink six-inch heart balloon. Tie the knot. Twist one of the lobes of the heart as shown, forming a two-inch bubble, and attach the beard assembly.

BALLOONS 3 AND 4 (BODY, ARMS, AND LEGS)

Inflate two red 260's, leaving about two to three inches of tail in each. Tie their knots and assemble as shown.

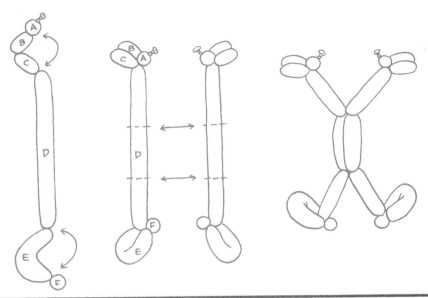

Attach Santa's head as shown.

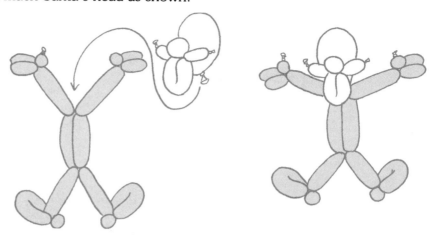

BALLOON 5 (SANTA'S COAT)

Inflate a white 260 a bit more than halfway. Tie the knot and attach to Santa's body as shown. Remove any excess balloon by using the safety bubble.

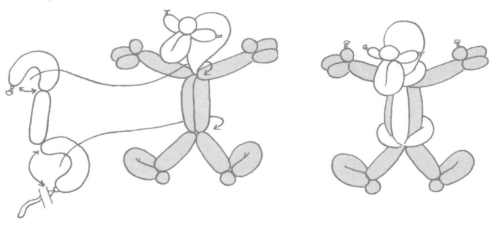

BALLOON 6

Inflate a red 260 leaving about an inch of tail. Tie the knot. Measure Santa's head and make a basic helmet. Add a twist at the top of the helmet to make the hat pointy.

BALLOON 7 (POM-POM)

Take a white, round balloon, or cut about three inches off the tip of a white 260. Inflate the round balloon or the 260 tip to the desired size.

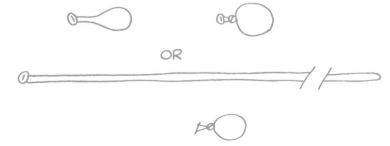

Tie the knot and attach as shown.

Jolly old Saint Nick is ready to deliver those toys! Oh, and a few candy canes too.

CANDY CANE

Candy Canes are fun balloon designs. They are easy to make, colorful and large, but don't bite them! Remember, balloons should go nowhere near your mouth.

This design requires two 260's, one red and one white. Inflate both fully and tie the knots. Lock both together as shown.

Twist the balloons around each other forming a spirallike post, then lock both balloons at the end as shown. If one balloon is longer than the other, twist the longer side at a tighter angle so that the balloons end more evenly.

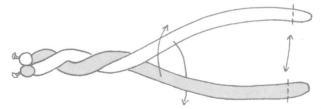

Twisting the balloon in the direction of the spiral, bend the post downward. Use the heat from your hands to help form the Cane by rubbing over the area of the bend.

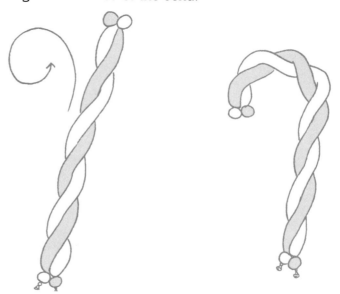

CANDY CANE HAT WITH BEAR

If you want to dress up your Candy Cane a bit, you can do so by adding a Teddy Bear. A green Bear will really compliment the red and white stripes. Then you can add the whole design to a hat by attaching as shown.

WREATH

The twist that forms the Candy Cane can also be used for a Wreath. Use green balloons for the spiral and connect at the ends. Use a red 260 to make a bow.

     Inflate the balloon leaving about two inches of tail, tie the knot, and assemble as shown.

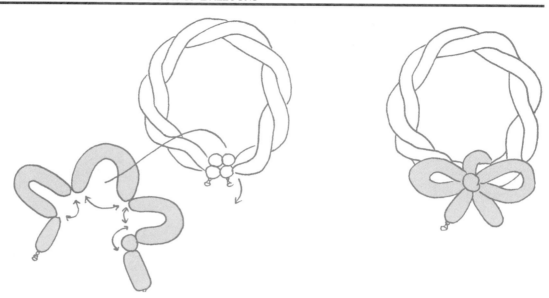

For a fuller wreath, use a braid as described in the July pages. Connect the ends and add a bow.

OUTLINE CHRISTMAS TREE

Finally, Christmas just wouldn't seem like Christmas without a Christmas Tree. I find that there are two successful approaches to creating a Christmas Tree with balloons. Each approach can be embellished to make bigger or smaller trees, depending on the direction you wish to take. I refer to these two styles as "Outline" and "Cluster."

The Outline Tree is exactly that: an outline that forms the shape of a Christmas tree. The example below is made of two green 260's.

BALLOON 1

Inflate the first balloon leaving about a half-inch of tail. Lock the ends together to form a loop. Find the top of the loop and make a twist —this will be the top of the tree.

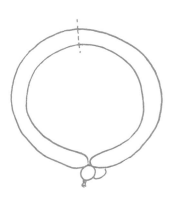 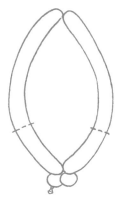

From the bottom, find a point about a quarter of the way up each side of the balloon, and make another twist on each side as shown.

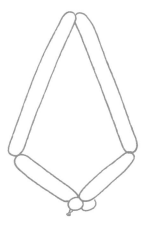

BALLOON 2

Inflate balloon two, leaving about three inches of tail, and tie the knot. Attach the balloon to the top of balloon 1 as shown. Hold balloon 1 and form it with your hands into a triangle (it will initially look more like a diamond). Lock balloon 2 in place as shown, and it will hold balloon 1 in shape. Finish balloon 2 as shown. Your tree should be able to stand on its own.

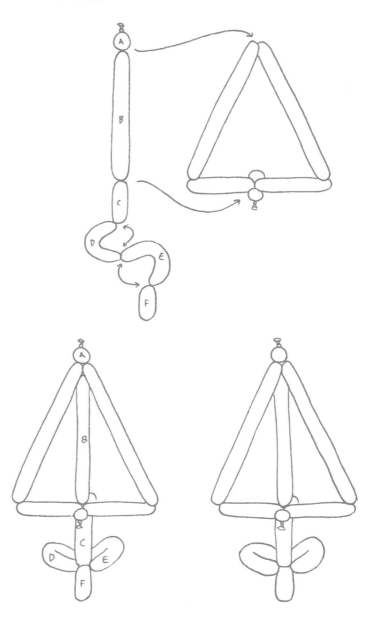

A fuller Outline Tree can be made by repeating the steps for balloon 1 so that three triangles are formed. The initial loop of each should be tied at the ends, instead of locked. Once formed, lock the triangles. Lock them together at the top and bottom, and add balloon 4.

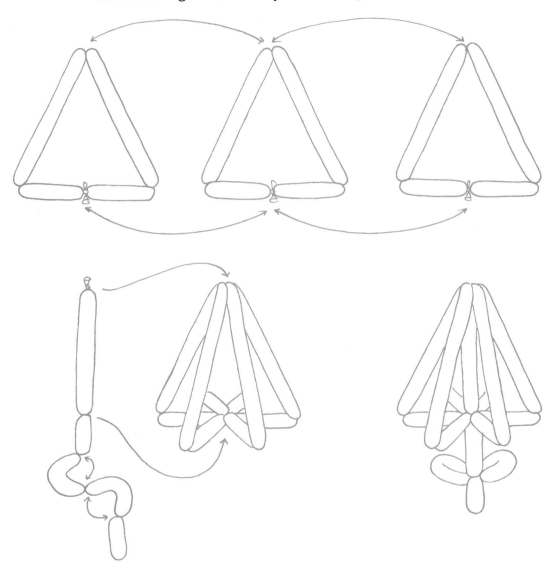

You can decorate your tree by adding inflated tips of 260's. Inflate the tip, tie the knots, and attach it with rubber cement, two-sided tape, or a cool-melt glue gun. Uninflated balloons can be used as garland.

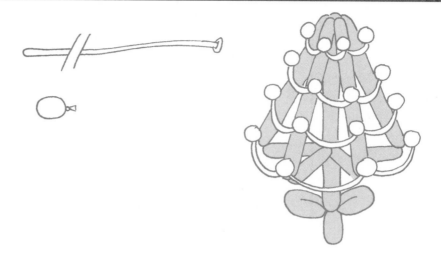

You can top off your tree with a small star. Inflate a 260 halfway and tie the knot. Complete the star as shown. Remove any excess by using the safety bubble, and attach it to the top of the tree by twisting the knot into the top of the point.

You now have a completely decorated Outline Christmas Tree!

CLUSTER CHRISTMAS TREE

The Cluster Christmas Tree is made by making clusters of branches that create levels on the tree. Starting at the top, each cluster gets larger as you work toward the bottom of the tree. The size of the tree depends on the number of levels you make. This will also determine the number of balloons used.

Start at the top with one green 260 that is inflated a bit more than halfway. Tie the knot and form two small ear twists. This will create a "seat" for your star. Make a one-inch bubble that will be your level spacer, and make a cluster of three ear twists and another one-inch spacer bubble. Make three larger ear twists and another spacer. On the next level you will make three fold twists that are a bit bigger than the previous ear twists and another spacer. You should be able to make at least one more level, using larger ear twists as you go.

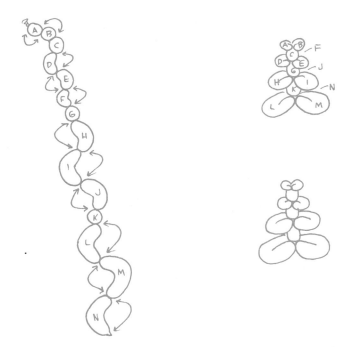

Start your next level by inflating another green 260, this time leaving about four inches of tail. Tie the knot. Start with a spacer, then make a wider cluster of fold twists, this time using four fold twists in the cluster. Lock to the top of the tree as shown. Make a spacer and continue to work down in levels of four fold twists, each larger than the last. Use as many balloons as you wish to achieve the desired size of your tree, always ending each balloon at a spacer and removing any excess balloon with a safety bubble and tie a knot.

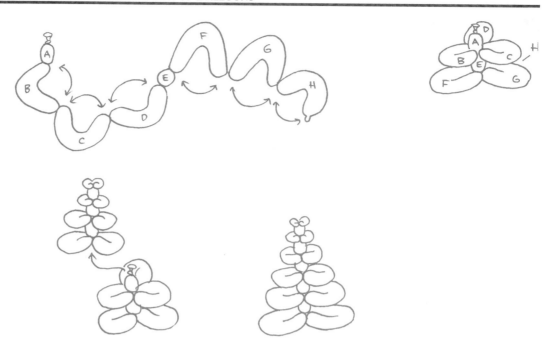

Finally, make a base as shown, and attach it to the bottom of the tree.

Add decorations as shown on the Outline Tree. On this tree, it is possible to tuck the knots of the inflated tips into the fold twists to attach ornaments. Garland can be added in this manner as well.

For those of you that are *really* daring, you can even add lights. Just don't let them burn long enough to get hot.

Chapter Fourteen
Year-Round Celebrations

The calendar helps us plan our holidays throughout the year, and though most holidays fall on either the same date or the same general time of year, some very joyous occasions can happen at any time. Some, like birthdays and anniversaries are celebrated yearly, while others are one-timers, like weddings, baby showers, and retirements. As a clown, I can tell you firsthand that people never get tired of celebrating. I get called on every day to entertain at somebody's party, for all kinds of occasions, and I never get tired of seeing all those happy faces!

Balloons are always a big part of every party, although some parties don't have a specific image or subject matter that might inspire a design. In fact, sometimes balloons just as balloons can be the perfect thing.

BIRTHDAY HAT

For birthdays, anniversaries, and retirements, balloon hats are always fun. I usually like to make a huge hat for birthday celebrants. It requires seven balloons and is about five feet tall when finished.

Six of the balloons are fully inflated 260's of the wearer's favorite colors. The last balloon is either a six-inch heart or a round balloon.

Use the diagram to construct this hat, which is built on a basic helmet.

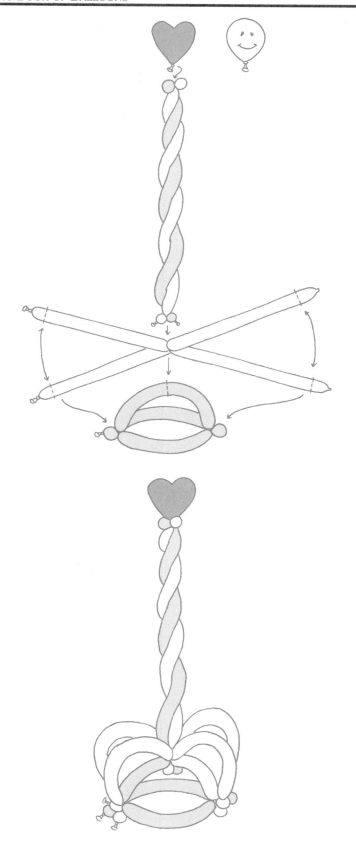

ANNIVERSARY HAT FOR TWO

Wedding anniversaries require a romantic design. Any design from our Valentine's Day collection would be fine, but I feel that anniversaries are about a long-lasting, durable union between two people who love each other. To celebrate this union, I've come up with a fitting hat. It is easy to do and large enough to light up a room. Whenever I put this hat on two love birds, I always receive a great reaction from any onlookers.

This hat requires four 260's, each inflated with about a half-inch tail. Tie each knot.

Make basic helmets out of the first two 260's, measuring the wearers, fitting one to the wife and the other to the husband.

Connect the two hats by lock twisting each end of the third balloon to a helmet as shown.

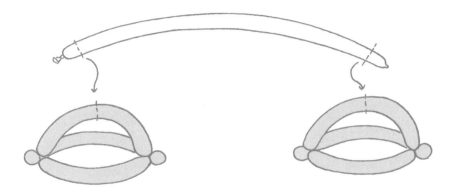

Make a heart shape out of the remaining balloon by locking the ends together to form a loop and squeezing it into shape with your hand, as we learned with our Valentine's designs.

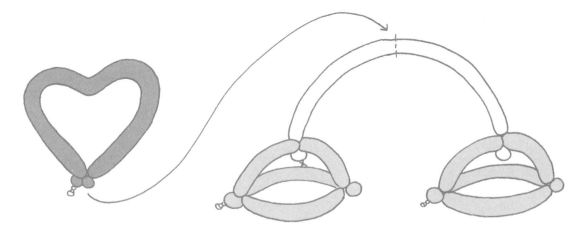

Attach the heart to the center of the connecting balloon by locking it in place as shown, then join your two lovers together by placing the helmets on their heads.

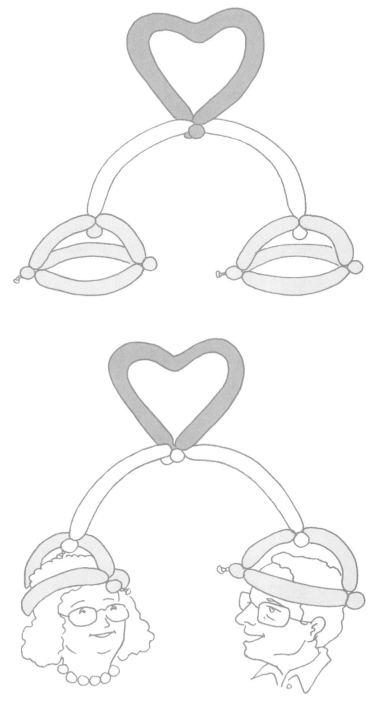

RETIREMENT HAIR HAT

Retirements usually require a little more creativity on the balloon artist's part. It can be a good idea to create a design that is based on the type of work the person did. This leaves us open to a multitude of possibilities.

Sometimes it is helpful to get ideas from other things. A good example is that a lot of older men who are retiring are also balding, so a fun hat to make may be a Big Hair Hat. This is simple to make and usually gets a big laugh. Be sure that the potential wearer has a good sense of humor about his hair, so he does not consider the hat an insult.

This hat is built on a basic helmet. Simply take a number of fully inflated 260's (four or five is an average amount), join them together by twisting them at their centers, and then lock them at this point to the top of the helmet as shown.

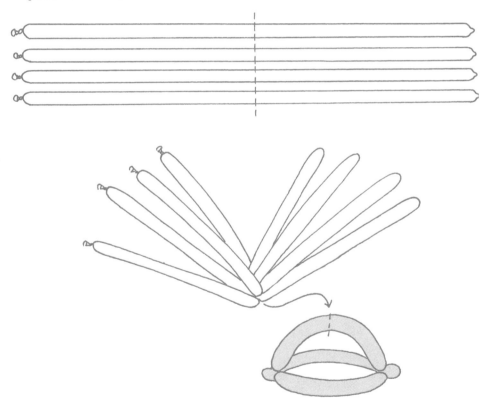

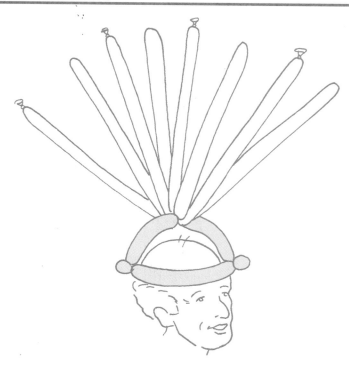

BRIDAL OR BABY SHOWER UMBRELLA

Weddings and births are usually preceded by a celebration known as a shower where women usually gather and shower the wife-to-be or mother-to-be with gifts. The title shower has inspired many to use umbrellas as part of the theme of the party. Umbrellas are fun to make with balloons, though they stop very little rain. The following is a beautiful umbrella that is great for these types of celebrations.

This design requires five 260's and seven six-inch hearts.

Inflate three 260's, leaving about a half-inch tail on each, and tie their knots.

Find the center of each and lock them all together at this point.

You now have six ribs for your umbrella. At the halfway point on each rib, make a one-inch ear twist. Once you have made an ear twist in each rib, connect lock the end of each rib to the ear twist of the rib next to it as shown.

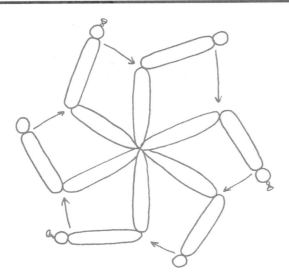

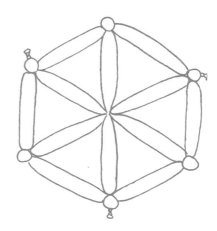

Inflate the remaining two 260's fully, and tie their knots. Lock them together at the end, and make a two-balloon twist as you did for the Candy Cane back in December. Lock the other end and attach to the center of the umbrella by locking the end bubbles around the center point of the ribs.

Inflate the six-inch hearts and tie their knots. Attach them to the umbrella as shown by locking their knots into the locked points of the umbrella. You can consider adding a teddy or other animal to add dimension or color to your design. This could be a great opportunity to personalize the design for the honoree.

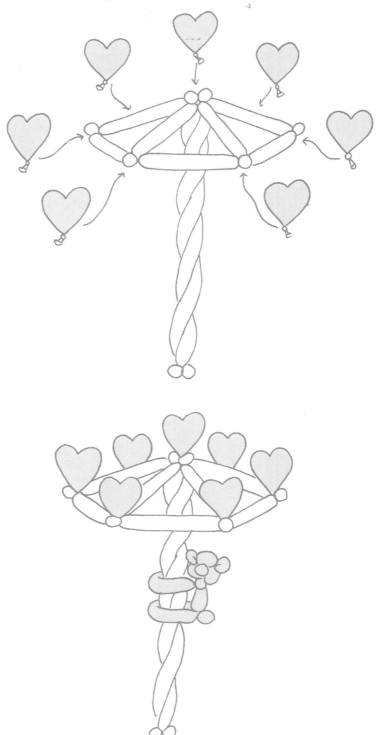

You can see what a beautiful design the umbrella is. Use color to be more specific for each celebration. For weddings, use white balloons with clear six-inch hearts for a spectacular and lacy look. Red hearts can also be used.

For baby showers use pastel colors. Pink, baby blue, yellow, white, and clear are all good choices. You can be more specific if the gender of the baby is known.

STORK WITH A SPECIAL DELIVERY

Another great design for baby showers, and baby births for that matter, is a Stork delivering a baby. It can be made with four 260's.

BALLOON 1 (THE HEAD, NECK AND BODY)

Inflate a white 260, leaving about four inches of tail, and tie the knot. Assemble as shown.

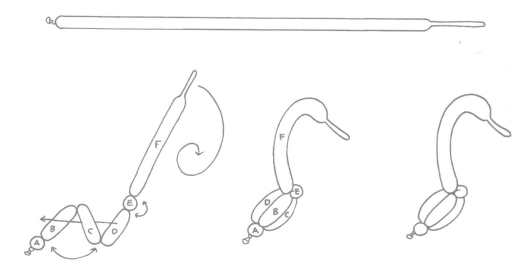

BALLOON 2

Inflate an orange 260, leaving about a half-inch tail, and tie the knot. Make three-inch bubbles and a one-inch ear twist on each end as shown. These are the legs.

Find the center point of this assembly, and make a joint. Attach it to balloon 1 as shown.

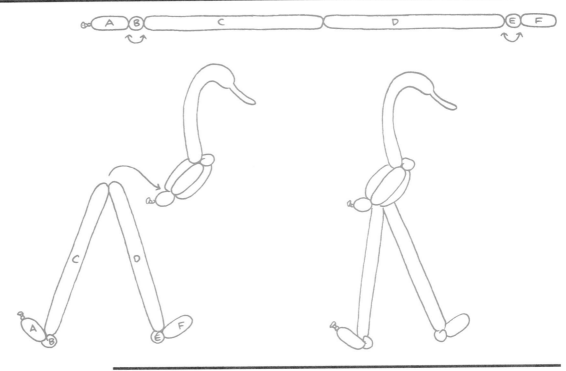

BALLOON 3

Inflate either a pink or a baby-blue 260, leaving about four inches of tail. Tie the knot and assemble as shown, removing any excess balloon using the safety bubble. This is the baby basket.

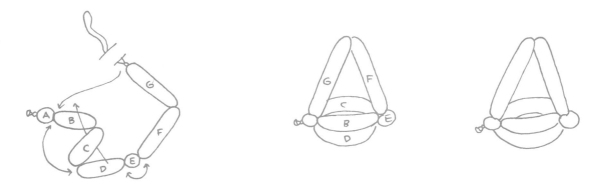

BALLOON 4

Inflate about four or five inches of a white balloon and tie the knot. Starting with the knot of the balloon, make an ear twist. Make a three-inch bubble, remove excess balloon using the safety bubble, and tie a knot. This is the baby. Insert the baby into the basket as shown.

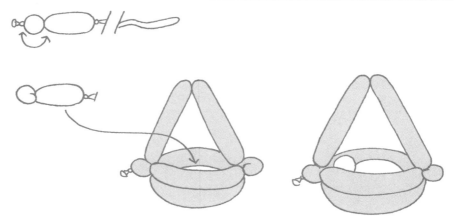

Attach the basket to the tip of the stork's bill by pinching it over the end as shown. Add markings with a permanent marker for a finished effect.

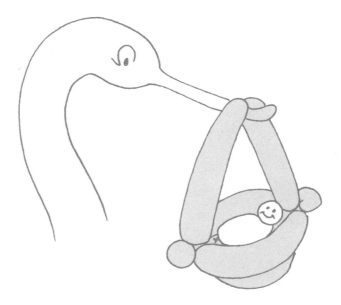

You can attach the stork to a helmet by locking the heels of its feet together, then locking them onto a helmet a shown.

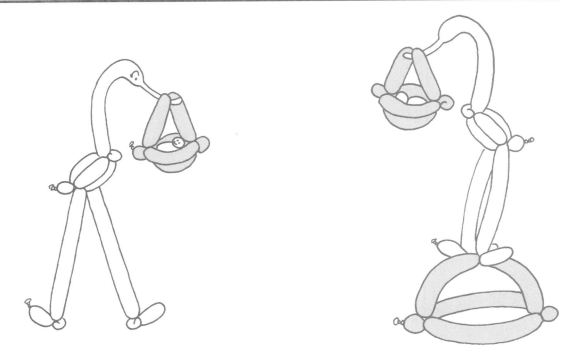

This little Stork will be a big hit at any baby shower!

THE LAST WORD

There seems to be no limit to what can be designed with balloons. As each day goes by, I seem to learn some new design or get a new idea from an old one. In this book we really just skimmed the surface of what it is possible to make for the holidays of the year, much like my previous book *Captain Visual's Big Book of Balloon Art,* with over one hundred designs in it, just opened the door for creative possibilities with balloons.

My goal with any of my books is to get the reader to realize that the printed ideas are there to get them started as balloon artists. There is no right or wrong way to make any design if the result resembles what it is intended to be. Exercise your creative muscles by learning the designs in this book. Keep your mind open to your own ideas, and add them to the ideas in this book. Expand on these concepts to create new ones, and I can guarantee that you will never look at balloons the same way again. In the future, you will look at a balloon as a painter looks at a canvas or a sculptor looks at a slab of marble.

No matter how far you get as a balloon artist, even if making a puppy is the limit of your skills, I thank you for expressing some interest in this unique craft. Above all, I hope you had fun playing with balloons, because when you get right down to it, fun is what balloons are really all about.

Have fun twistin'!

SUPPLIERS

T. Meyer's Magic
1509 Parker Bend
Austin, TX 78734
(512) 263-2313

M.E. Persson Clown Supplies
The Castles, Route 101
Suite C-7
Brentwood, NH 03833
(603) 679-3311

Clown City
509 Norwich Avenue
Taftville, CT 06380
(860) 889-1000

Mecca Magic
49 Dodd Street
Bloomfield, NJ 07003
(201) 429-7597

Daytona Magic
136 S. Beach Street
Daytona Beach, FL 32114
(800) 346-2442

To order *Captain Visual's Big Book of Balloon Art: A Complete Book of Balloonology for Beginners and Advanced Twisters* (#51641), call toll-free 1-800-477-BOOK (MasterCard or Visa), or send a check or money order (payable in U.S. funds) for $15.95, plus $5.00 shipping and handling, to Carol Publishing Group, Dept. CVB, 120 Enterprise Avenue, Secaucus, NJ 07094. (Book subject to availability; price subject to change.)